THE COMPLETE
AGA COOKBOOK

THE COMPLETE
AGA COOKBOOK

OVER 150 RECIPES FOR EVERY KIND OF OVEN

MARY BERRY & LUCY YOUNG

headline

First published in Great Britain in 2015 by
HEADLINE PUBLISHING GROUP

1

Cataloguing in Publication Data is available from the British Library

Hardback 9781472222640

Comissioning editor: Muna Reyal
Project editor: Jo Roberts-Miller
Design and art direction: Smith & Gilmour
Photographer: Georgia Glynn Smith
Assitant photographer: Bobbie Goulding
Food Stylist: Ellie Jarvis
Assistant food stylists: Danielle Sanchez and Elayna Rudolphy
Prop Stylist: Jenny Iggleden

Printed and bound in Germany by Mohn Media

Headline's policy is to use papers that are natural, renewable and
recyclable products and made from wood grown in sustainable forests.
The logging and manufacturing processes are expected to conform
to the environmental regulations of the country of origin.

HEADLINE PUBLISHING GROUP
An Hachette UK Company
Carmelite House
50 Victoria Embankment
London EC4Y 0DZ

www.headline.co.uk
www.hachette.co.uk

CONTENTS

INTRODUCTION

WELCOME TO THE WORLD OF AGA, A BRITISH ICONIC CAST IRON RANGE COOKER INVENTED IN THE 1920S.

TODAY'S AGA COOKERS

There is a wide choice of Aga cookers available today, to suit a variety of lifestyles, whether you want a cooker on all the time to provide background heat or one you can turn on and off as you need to use it; or indeed if you want something that sits between the two. They all work on the same principle of storing heat in the cast iron and each cooking area is pre-set to a different heat.

This book, its recipes and instructions, are generic to all models, so it should be used in conjunction with the user's guide supplied with your own cooker.

THE TRADITIONAL AGA COOKER

These models were originally solid fuel, but are now only available powered by gas, oil or electricity. Once they are commissioned they take around 7–12 hours to gain the full saturation of heat in their castings and are designed to run continuously. The single, relatively small, heat source means that the hotplates and ovens are all on together and there is constant warmth in the kitchen. Selected gas and electric models may have a programming facility.

THE AGA TOTAL CONTROL AND CITY60 COOKERS

Our latest models combine the design and values of the traditional Aga cooker with the ability to turn each cooking area off and on as your needs require, adjusting to your lifestyle. The ovens and hotplate(s) have individual controls. You can use the hotplate(s) independently of the ovens, or together with 1, 2, 3, 4 or 5 ovens, depending on the model, as your cooking requires. You must allow enough time for the castings to become saturated in heat though, do not be tempted to cook as soon as it is turned on!

THE AGA DUAL CONTROL

This model is powered by gas or electricity and has ovens which are permanently all on, as with the traditional models, and there is always gentle warmth in the kitchen. The hotplates have elements embedded underneath so can be independently operated and used together, or individually, as needed.

THE SECRET OF AGA COOKING — HOW YOUR AGA COOKER WORKS

The principle of using cast iron to accumulate and store heat is the basis on which the Aga works.

The Aga cooker is an outstandingly efficient energy store, steadily transferring the heat from its core, or from elements embedded in the cast iron, into its ovens and hotplates. Heat is transferred into the cast iron ovens and released steadily from all the inner surfaces simultaneously. Radiant energy, an infra-red heat, is produced from a heated mass and doesn't depend on hot oven air for transmission. In cooking, the absorption of the radiant heat seals the surface of the food, holding in the flavours and moisture. In an Aga cooker, the oven *is* the heat source. The cast iron sides, back, top and bottom, provide constant heat.

The ovens are large, able to take a 13kg (28 lb) turkey. Seven Aga saucepans, with flat lids, can be stacked in the Simmering Oven.

The Aga also emits gentle warmth and is often used as a heat source in the kitchen, as well as for cooking, where it is somewhat of a people magnet let alone a comforter for pets.

No matter which Aga cooker you have, it will produce great tasting food cooked with the radiant heat of cast iron. With all Aga cookers there are often several ways of producing the same results, as any meeting of Aga owners will confirm. The Total Control and City60 may cook some dishes slightly differently from the other models but the end result will ultimately look and taste the same.

KNOWING YOUR AGA

THE HOTPLATES

There are two cooking hotplates on all Aga cookers – one at a high heat, called the Boiling Plate, the other at a gentler heat, the Simmering Plate (apart from the Aga City60 which has one hotplate with a variable heat setting making it either a Boiling or Simmering Plate).

As the whole of the traditional Aga cooker is heated by a single heat source, the 80:20 rule applies – cook 20 per cent of the time on the hotplates and carry out most of the cooking in the ovens, such as steaming root vegetables or starting off a casserole or curry on the top then placing it in the Simmering Oven to cook. That way you ensure the most efficient use of the stored heat.

The Total and Dual Control and the City60 Aga cookers have separate electric elements underneath the cast iron hotplates so each of these models is designed to replenish itself constantly when it needs to so you can cook for the total cooking time on the top if the ovens are not turned on, should you wish. If you have had a traditional Aga cooker and change to hotplates that are independently operated be aware the hotplates may seem cooler initially but the heat is constantly maintained so they retain a steady heat which does not fall. Needless to say these hotplates do not affect the heat of the ovens.

BOILING PLATE

The hottest hotplate, the Boiling Plate is used for boiling, stir frying, making toast, using the griddle pan – indeed anything that requires a high heat. It is of a large diameter and can fit three average-sized saucepans together. Green vegetables keep their colour when boiled quickly here. When stir frying or cooking anything that might splash, we would recommend using an Aga Splash Shield which will protect the insulated cover liner from splatter, making cleaning a doddle! Please bear in mind that the Boiling Plate is too hot to cook food directly on it.

SIMMERING PLATE

The Simmering Plate is the cooler of the two hotplates and is used for recipes that require a lower heat, such as making sauces, scrambling eggs, heating milk, slow frying, simmering soups and root vegetables. In addition it can be used directly as a form of griddle – invaluable for toasted sandwiches, quesadillas, drop scones, searing scallops or even a fried egg (you will need to cover the plate with Bake-O-Glide, or other non-stick silicone paper)! Slow cooked toast can be made directly on the Simmering Plate – no need to use the Aga toaster. The same size as the Boiling Plate, the Simmering Plate is also machined flat to give the best all-over contact with the Aga saucepans, grill pan, frying pan and kettle.

WARMING PLATE

This is available on 4 and 5 oven Aga cookers. This oblong plate is a useful spot for placing hot dishes straight from the oven, resting cooked meat and poultry, serving from or warming the tea pot or sauce boats and jugs. It's great, too, for keeping coffee warm, airing clothes, 'ironing' tea towels or drying off items such as peelers or food processor blades.

THE TOP PLATE

The top plate is the enamelled surface surrounding the hotplates. Although it is not a cooking surface you can use its warmth for a number of useful activities, which more often than not save time and washing-up! These include warming jars of honey or syrup, melting butter or chocolate in a basin – do please put the basin on a cork mat or folded piece of kitchen towel to avoid scratching the enamel. Although it is a durable and hard-wearing surface, vitreous enamel is glass and will show scratch marks.

The top plate can also be used to rest a cup of coffee or tea or dry off awkwardly shaped tins, peelers or food mixer and processor parts – again use protection if you want to keep your Aga pristine!

THE WARMING PLATE

THE HOTPLATES

BOILING PLATE

SIMMERING PLATE

WHICH MODEL IS YOURS?

The Aga cooker comes in a range of sizes with a differing number of ovens. Search the descriptions below to find your own cooker and refer to the user's instructions supplied with your new cooker, or available online at **agaliving.com** under Technical Library, for a bespoke description and advice.

2 OVEN AGA COOKERS

There are two models in this range, the traditional **Aga** with one single heat source, on all the time. It has a Roasting Oven and a Simmering Oven. The new **Aga City60** has been designed to have all the attributes of a larger Aga within a small space. Each area is independently heated so they can be used together or in isolation. The single hotplate has two settings, so can be either a Boiling or Simmering Plate with a specially designed Resting Area to extend usage. The top oven also has two settings; so it can be either a Roasting or Baking Oven. The lower oven is the Simmering Oven. Flat floor grids are provided to use when cooking on the floor of the ovens.

3 OVEN AGA COOKERS

In this family there are the **Aga Total Control** and the **Aga Dual Control**, plus the traditional gas and electric models. The principles of cooking are the same for all; however, the Total Control gives greater flexibility as each area can be turned on and off as required. Compared to the traditional Aga, heat-up time is fast, generally an hour for best performance. The Total Control is designed for households that do not want constant warmth or are away from home for long periods – of course in colder spells or for convenience the Total Control can be left on like the traditional model. There is a floor grid for use when cooking for a period of time directly on the floor of the ovens. The Aga Dual Control has traditional Aga ovens always available for use but has hotplates that may be switched on and off.

4 OVEN AGA COOKERS

The 4 oven Aga cookers are all of the traditional type with one heat source and are a constant means of warming the kitchen and can be always available for use. These Aga cookers use the established techniques where most of the cooking is undertaken in the ovens, the hotplates being used to start food cooking.

5 OVEN AGA COOKERS

The 5 oven Aga is essentially a 3 oven Aga with an attached independently controlled hotcupboard unit on the left-hand side. As there is already a Simmering Oven featured in this model, the extra oven is a Slow Cooking Oven, which operates in a similar way, albeit at a slightly lower heat – this permits long periods of slow cooking. The 5 oven Aga is available as a Total Control or a Dual Control. The wealth of ovens makes this Aga especially brilliant for entertaining or for larger families.

THE AGA CITY60

2 OVEN AGA

3 OVEN AGA

4 OVEN AGA

5 OVEN AGA

OVEN FUNCTIONS

ROASTING OVEN

The Roasting Oven is very hot, wonderful for cooking meat and poultry, roast potatoes and other vegetables, crispy jacket potatoes, grilled foods, pastry and bread.

The Roasting Oven is zoned in heat, meaning it is slightly hotter towards the top than the centre and the oven grid shelf set on the oven floor is less hot than the centre.

The top of the oven, second runners down, is great for grilled breakfasts and browning dishes such as gratins. The middle of the oven is best for roast meats and scones; tarts, quiches and bread are better near the floor of the oven.

The Roasting Oven is excellent for bread and pastries. Quiches in ceramic or pies in Pyrex dishes don't need to be baked blind as when they are placed on the floor of the oven the pastry cooks from underneath and the filling will set and brown from the all-round heat. Metal flan tins conduct heat quicker than ceramic so put them on the oven grid shelf placed on the floor of the oven to avoid over-browning on the base of the food.

The floor of the oven can be used as another cooking surface; indeed, it is often called a hidden hotplate. It is ideal for browning roast potatoes, sautéing cubes of meat for a casserole or completing the cooking of grilled chicken fillets in a cast iron grill pan. As it is indirectly heated, the floor of the Roasting Oven is also great for cooking pizzas.

The Aga Total Control and the City60 come with an oven floor grid. This should be used when cooking anything on the City60 oven floor and when cooking on the floor of the Total Control for more than 20 minutes. This is because the element is positioned in the floor of the oven.

The beauty of the Roasting Oven is that any fat splashes are burnt off when the oven is at full heat. Just brush it out occasionally to get rid of carbon deposits.

The specially designed roasting tins and bakeware slide directly on to the runners, so almost every available square centimetre of space can be used. Food can be protected by the use of the cold plain shelf or shielded by using the large roasting tin, which means that you can cook food that requires different temperatures at the same time. If food is browning too quickly just slide the cold plain shelf over the food to reduce the top heat. This oven can also be used for moderate baking by using the cold plain shelf as a shield above the food, such as when baking a traybake.

BAKING OVEN

The Baking Oven is pre-set at a moderate heat, ideal for cakes, biscuits and other foods not requiring a high temperature.

As with the Roasting Oven there are heat zones within the oven, the top is slightly hotter than the bottom and this will affect the positioning of the foods. In general small cakes and lasagne are cooked towards the top; baked fish, crumbles and meringue roulades around the centre and Victoria sandwiches, loaf cakes and biscuits on the oven grid shelf placed on the floor of the oven.

Many items cooked in the Roasting Oven can be cooked in the Baking Oven but for a longer time, such as meat and poultry. A turkey can be cooked here either for the whole time or after starting it off for an hour in the Roasting Oven. To prevent the over-browning of larger cakes, slide the plain shelf on to the second set of runners when the perfect colour has been achieved.

SIMMERING OVEN

The Simmering Oven is pre-set at a gentle heat, ideal for long, slow cooking. It is best described as a continuation oven, as it continues to cook food that has been brought up to heat elsewhere on the cooker – with the exception of meringues which are dried out rather than 'cooked'.

Root vegetables can be steamed to perfection here; simply bring to the boil for a few minutes, drain off all the water, cover the saucepan with a lid then steam in the oven until tender – the time will depend on the size of the vegetable. Wonderful stocks for a soup or risotto can also be produced in this oven, as can slow-roasted meats and perfect steamed Basmati rice every time.

The same size as the other Aga ovens the Simmering Oven can take up to seven Aga saucepans, stacked to make best use of the space and this certainly extends the cooking capacity, so useful when cooking for crowds.

Aga City60 owners should use their oven floor grid when cooking on the floor of the Simmering Oven.

NOTE TO AGA TOTAL CONTROL OWNERS:
When the Roasting and Baking Oven are in the Slumber mode they can also be used as a Simmering Oven; in fact a rich fruit cake cooked in one of these ovens on Slumber gives excellent results.

SLOW COOKING OVEN
The addition of a Slow Cooking Oven is perfect for large families, those who enjoy entertaining or anyone who simply loves to cook. It is at a slightly lower heat than the Simmering Oven and it can be used in much the same way but for a longer cooking time.

This oven is ideal for dishes such as shoulder or leg of lamb, steamed puddings, casseroles and stocks. The Slow Cooking Oven and the Warming Oven are a separate electric unit (known as a hotcupboard), attached to the 3 oven Aga and this unit operates independently of the parent Aga via a switch.

WARMING OVEN
Perfect for warming plates and serving dishes, this oven has many more uses: keeping covered meals warm for the late-comer, resting meat before carving,

holding sauces (the sauce can be placed in a jug then covered with clingfilm – the oven heat is gentle so don't worry). It can keep cooked food hot for up to two hours before serving.

The Warming Oven is great for drying out individual meringues, which keep their whiteness, about 2½ hours for a tray of meringues.

The gentle heat here acts rather like a dehydrator and can be used for drying banana chips, apple rings, tomatoes, mushrooms or even grapes to make your own raisins.

MODULE OPTION
The Module is a conventional cooker in the style of an Aga, attached to the parent Aga. It is a separate unit and independently operated. The Module is used as other conventional cookers.

THE HEAT INDICATOR
The Heat Indicator is present on selected models positioned above the Roasting Oven, incorporated on the handset on programmable models, or situated behind the control door (or possibly not present at all, as with the City60).

The purpose of the Heat Indicator is to show whether or not the cooker as a whole contains the full amount of stored heat with which to start cooking; it is not an oven thermometer. Exact temperatures are not so important when cooking with the radiant heat of cast iron; it cooks differently from using just hot air and is kinder to food.

It is quite normal for the Heat Indicator to register an apparent fall in heat, when cooking, so do not worry – the Aga automatically restores itself. The Heat Indicator plate is 'graded' where applicable.

The Heat Indicator used to show a mercury line but since 2010 this has no longer been available due to legislation.

AGA EQUIPMENT SUPPLIED WITH YOUR COOKER

FULL SIZE ROASTING TIN WITH GRILL RACK

This is designed to slide on to the oven runners without needing to sit on an oven grid shelf. The roasting tin can be used with the grill rack, in its high position, for grilling at the top of the Roasting Oven. It can be used for roasting meat or poultry with or without the grill rack. Large quantities of roast potatoes can be cooked in this tin and it can also be used to make large traybakes or cakes. The grill rack is effective on its own as a cake cooking rack. The roasting tin can be used in any oven but is not recommended for hotplate use.

HALF SIZE ROASTING TIN AND GRILL RACK

Designed for sliding on to the oven runners widthways or to be sat on an oven grid shelf. The half size roasting tin can be used with the grill rack, in its high position, for grilling at the top of the Roasting Oven. It can be used for roasting smaller joints of meat or poultry with or without the grill rack. Roast potatoes can be cooked in this tin. The roasting tin can also be employed for making traybakes or cakes. The grill rack is useful on its own as a cake cooking rack. As above, it can be used in any oven but is not recommended for hotplate use.

OVEN GRID SHELVES

These are for inserting in each oven to provide a surface for dishes and tins which do not fit direct onto the oven runners. They can be used in any oven, as required.

THE PLAIN SHELF

More often this is known as the Cold Plain Shelf, as it should be kept out of the ovens when not in use. It has two uses: one as a large baking sheet for scones, biscuits, pastry and meringues; the other as a heat deflector to reduce the top heat if food is overbrowning before it is cooked through.

TOASTER

This is for toasting bread on the Boiling Plate. Aga toast is renowned for its excellence, crisp on the outside and soft in the centre. Take thick slices of bread and place in the Aga toaster – if the bread is very moist or very fresh, heat the toaster beforehand to prevent sticking – lift the Boiling Plate insulated cover and place the toaster direct on to the plate with the handle at an angle from the handle of the cover. Close the cover and wait for the bread to toast on one side – this will take 1–2 minutes depending on the variety of bread – open the cover and turn the toaster over and repeat the process to toast the other side. The toaster can also be used for heating pitta bread and toasting teacakes.

WIRE BRUSH

This is for cleaning the raw cast iron surfaces, keeping them clear of crumbs and burnt-on debris – which would otherwise affect the boiling performance of pans and the kettle. Use on the hotplates and the ovens. Take care not to touch the enamel surfaces as the wire brush will scratch the finish.

FLOOR GRID

This shelf is supplied with the Total Control and City60 for cooking on the floor of the ovens; it protects food from the fluctuation of heat from the base element.

CARING FOR YOUR AGA

Your Aga cooker is easy to keep clean and just a little care will keep it gleaming like new. One of the really good things about an Aga is that it does not need much attention as the ovens and hotplates will, over a period of time, carbonise fat splashes and spills.

TOP PLATE AND FRONT PLATE

The easiest way to clean the Aga top plate and front plate is to mop up spills as soon as they happen. It is useful to keep a damp cloth handy to do this. Baked-on food is more difficult to clean but can usually be removed with the Aga vitreous enamel cleaner using a damp cloth, or, if necessary, a nylon scouring pad. If milk or fruit juice or anything containing acid is spilt on the cooker, wipe it up immediately. Also clean off any condensation streaks on the front plate around the oven doors or the vitreous enamel may be permanently discoloured.

All that is usually needed to keep the vitreous enamel surfaces of the cooker bright and clean is a daily rub over with a damp soapy cloth followed immediately with a clean, dry cloth to avoid streaks. The Aga E-cloths are excellent for this.

Remember the top plate and the polished stainless steel insulated covers will scratch if pans or utensils are dragged across them.

INSULATING COVERS AND OVEN DOOR LININGS

The best way to keep the linings clean is to wipe them over after cooking so that splashes do not get baked on (taking care with a hot cooker). The use of a Splash Shield to keep the linings free from baked-on fat splashes will also help. Clean the linings when they are cool, or the cooker is off.

Oven door linings can be cleaned with hot soapy water and/or a cream cleanser. To deep clean the linings, place a towel on the work surface, carefully lift off the oven door (doors are heavy) and place it enamel side down on the towel padding. Clean with a soapy impregnated pad to remove stubborn marks. Do not immerse the doors in water as they are packed with insulating material which will be damaged by excessive moisture. Needless to say, do not put oven doors in a dishwasher! Dry off before carefully replacing on their hinges.

The tops of the insulated covers (lids) are stainless steel and can be kept clean by wiping over with a damp cloth and polished up. The Aga E-cloths are excellent for this purpose as they are lint-free and eco-friendly.

OVENS

The ovens are made from cast iron, and are very durable. Under normal use they merely need to be brushed out occasionally with the wire brush supplied. The hot ovens burn off fat splashes during use. If the ovens on the new generation of Aga cookers show rusting, clean off with a wire brush then spray with a little corn oil.

HOTPLATES

The hotplates are easy to care for, and regular maintenance will ensure the best performance. Removing any crumbs or spills will mean the surface is kept flat to ensure complete contact with the base of pans and kettles. Should the hotplates need cleaning, use a sponge, cloth, scouring pad or the wire brush to remove burnt-on spills.

Hotplates are made from cast iron, and are very durable, but they will rust if left turned off for lengths of time, especially in moist conditions. If when you go on holiday you turn the Aga off, you could apply a thin coating of cooking oil when the hotplates are cold.

ROASTING TINS

The enamelled roasting tins supplied with the Aga should be cleaned in hot soapy water, soaking if necessary. A nylon scouring pad can also be used. They may also be cleaned in the dishwasher, but with constant use, the enamelled finish will become dull in appearance.

SERVICING YOUR AGA

To keep your Aga cooker running efficiently we recommend that it is regularly serviced by an Approved Aga engineer. Refer to the user's guide for the servicing intervals for your model. Approved Aga engineers have been factory trained and always use genuine Aga spares.

OLDER AGA COOKERS

If you have inherited an Aga or have an older one it may work differently from the new ones. The principles are the same but cooking times may vary. It's a case of getting used to your own individual cooker. Make a note of the time it takes for your Aga cooker to cook the recipes in this book so you know for the next time – in fact this is a good tip for us all.

RECONDITIONED AND CONVERTED AGA COOKERS

Reconditioned and converted Aga cookers can often be more problematic and may have been serviced using parts that are not genuine Aga materials. The oven temperatures may vary significantly from the way they were designed originally, making it difficult to get consistent cooking results. They also tend to be less fuel efficient and, as a general rule, caution is advised if considering a purchase.

USING THIS BOOK

➻ All the recipes have been tested with the Aga cooker at full normal heat, the Aga Total Control, City60 and any cooker with programmability at saturated heat

➻ Oven shelf positions are counted from the top down

➻ Exact temperature conversions are not possible – if converting your own recipe, look in the book for a similar one

➻ Detailed instructions for cooking on a 2 oven traditional Aga can be found with this sign ⚫ 2 oven

SHOW ME HOW

To make the most of your Aga cooker, go to an Aga Demonstration. Your local Aga shop will have details (see agaliving.com).

BREAKFAST
AND
LUNCH

Sunday Morning Breakfast

Whatever you choose to eat for breakfast, the Aga takes over. You need never stand over a spitting frying pan again. Instead, let the family prepare toast to their liking while an oven-grilled breakfast sizzles quietly in one tin in the oven. No smells, no mess. Good Morning!

This is all cooked in the large roasting tin. If cooking for one or two, use an Aga cast iron pan on the floor of the Roasting Oven. The quantities below are per person.

a little bacon fat
1 sausage
1 tomato, halved
2 rashers bacon
50g (2 oz) mushrooms, wiped
1 egg

1 Grease the large roasting tin with a little bacon fat and put the sausages at one end.

2 Hang the tin on the highest set of runners in the Roasting Oven and cook for about 10 minutes. Turn the sausages and cook again for about 10 minutes (5 will be enough for chipolatas).

3 Add the tomatoes, cut side up, and the rashers of bacon to the tin and cook for 5–7 minutes. Turn the bacon and sausages and cook for a further 5 minutes.

4 Add the mushrooms and cook for 5 minutes. If necessary add a little more bacon fat when turning the mushrooms.

5 Break the eggs into one end of the tin, put the tin on the floor of the oven and cook for a final 2–3 minutes. (You could also fry the eggs to order on silicone paper on the Simmering Plate – see photo opposite.)

PREPARE AHEAD
If you want to cook the sausages ahead, they can be kept warm in the Simmering Oven for up to an hour, but the rest is best cooked to serve.

CONVENTIONAL OVEN
Cook on the hob and under the grill in the usual way.

GRILLED BACON

Grilling is done in the Roasting Oven. Either use the grill rack in the roasting tin, hanging the tin from the highest set of runners, or put the bacon straight into the tin with the tin on the floor of the oven. Timing again is very variable – about 3 minutes each side for thin bacon and up to 7 minutes either side for thicker cuts.

GRILLED SAUSAGES

Again in the Roasting Oven – put sausages on to the grill rack in the roasting tin hung on the highest set of runners. Turn once.

OVEN FRIED BREAD

The timing for fried bread varies according to the thickness of the slices and also depends on whether the bread is brown or white (brown bread takes longer). Spread bacon fat or other fat on both sides of the bread and put into a roasting tin on the floor of the Roasting Oven, turning after about 5–7 minutes.

AGA TOAST

Using the special Aga toaster is easy as it does not matter how thick or thin the slices of bread are. You can toast at least four slices at a time according to the size of the loaf. Time varies according to the thickness of the slices and brown bread generally takes longer. Toast on the Boiling Plate leaving the lid up. For faster toast, put the lid down but watch it very carefully. This way is not quite so crisp.

FRIED EGGS ON THE TOP PLATES

A fried egg can easily be cooked quickly on the Simmering Plate of the Aga. Lift the lid of the plate for a couple of minutes before cooking, lay a piece of silicone paper on top and smear with butter, if liked (the photo on the previous page shows a Bake-O-Glide circle in use). Break an egg in a cup and tip on to the sizzling butter. To cook the yolk a little, close the lid. You will be able to fry 4 eggs on the plate at a time.

Kippers

No smells and delicious moist kippers
result from this method of cooking in the oven.

2 good knobs of butter
a pair of kippers
freshly ground black
    pepper

1 Put a knob of butter on top of each kipper and
sprinkle with black pepper. Wrap each one loosely
in foil, folding the foil over but not sealing it.
Place side by side in the small roasting tin.

2 Hang the tin on the lowest set of runners
in the Roasting Oven and cook for 15 minutes
or until cooked through.

PREPARE AHEAD
The kippers will keep in
the Simmering Oven for
up to an hour.

CONVENTIONAL OVEN
Bake in an oven preheated
to 220°C/Fan 200°C/Gas 7,
for about 15 minutes until
cooked through.

Porridge

So easy to make in the Aga. Lucy always cooks her
porridge with milk and serves it with blueberries and brown
sugar, while Mary prefers hers cooked with water and
served plain – traditional to her Scottish roots!

75g (3 oz) porridge oats
600ml (1 pint) milk
   or water

1 Measure the oats and milk or water into a small
pan. Heat on the Boiling Plate and stir until boiling.

2 Cover with a lid and transfer to the Simmering
Oven for about 5 minutes until all the liquid has
been absorbed and the porridge is cooked and soft.

PREPARE AHEAD
The porridge is best cooked
to serve.

CONVENTIONAL OVEN
Cook on the hob in the
usual way.

PRESERVES

The great thing about preserving is that the word describes the act so precisely. What could be more wonderful than locking away the fruits of a golden summer to enjoy throughout the winter? I find the whole process deeply satisfying.

EQUIPMENT

The heavy Aga preserving pan is most useful because it gives plenty of space for the jam to froth up when boiling, without boiling over. Pans should be only about half full. Even though I have a preserving pan, I still prefer to divide, say, a 5kg (11 lb) lot of marmalade into two batches when I reach the stage of boiling the fruit with the sugar. This means that it comes to a full rolling boil quickly and, as the pan is large, it froths up but cannot boil over. A good guide for those making jam and marmalade without a large preserving pan is not to make more than a 4kg (9 lb) yield in a 5.5 litre (10 pint) pan, or a 3kg (6 lb 8 oz) yield in an 4.5 litre (8 pint) pan.

The best choice of pan is stainless steel, heavy aluminium or heavy enamel. Brass and copper can be used but they reduce the vitamin C in the jam. Cast iron should not be used for preserving. The base of pans may be rubbed with a little butter to prevent sticking.

LIDS AND JARS

I find it a great bore to use discs of waxed paper on top of the jam or marmalade and cellophane tops and elastic bands. It is time consuming to do and after a few months the jam shrinks down the jar. Also, you have no proper lid once the jar is opened. I prefer to use screwtop lids on jam jars. The ideal ones are honey jars. The lids should be really clean. I gather the best jars through the year and store them with their lids ready. If you are a WI member where you have strict rules, you can buy new screw tops and snap on plastic lids for the older type of jars.

Warm jars at the back of the Aga or in the Simmering Oven before use. Cover jars when they are first potted and piping hot or when cold – never when warm.

SUGAR

Choose granulated sugar for economical jams and marmalades, but take care to stir constantly when it is added to the pan and dissolving. It forms a dense layer, prone to burn, on the bottom of the pan if heated without stirring.

Preserving sugar is more expensive, large grained and less prone to sticking on the bottom of the pan and so needs less stirring. It produces less scum and so a clearer jelly or jam. Choose this sugar for jelly jams and any special jam and marmalade you are making.

Jam sugar is a specially formulated sugar mixed with acid and pectin. It is ideal for fruits low in natural acid and/or pectin to give a perfect set. Use for Apricot, Blackberry, Elderberry, Cherry, Sweet Oranges, Pears, Peaches, Nectarines, Raspberry, Strawberry and Rhubarb. You may even use it to make cartons of fruit juice into quick and easy jelly jams, such as Pineapple, Apple, Grape and Tropical Fruits. All sugar can be warmed slightly in the Simmering Oven or on the back of the Aga before use to speed dissolving.

FRUIT

Firm fresh fruit that is slightly under- rather than over-ripe will give the best 'set' in jam. This is when the pectin level is at its highest. Most fruits need to be cooked gently and thoroughly before the sugar is added. Bring to the boil with water as given in the recipe, simmer on the top of the Aga for 5 minutes and then cover and continue to cook in the Simmering Oven until the fruit is pulpy.

If you are using frozen fruit, to ensure you have a good colour to the jam, cook the fruit straight from frozen, without thawing first. Use the same proportion of fruit and sugar as in other jams and marmalades.

TESTING FOR A GOOD SET

Overcooking causes jam to darken and lose flavour. Underboiling will give a runny jam. Three methods may be used to judge the best setting point.

1 Use a sugar or cooking thermometer to test the temperature in the centre of the pan – 105°C is a good setting point.

2 When a spoon of jam is allowed to cool a little and the jam falls in a 'flake' or large droplet from the edge of the spoon.

3 When a spoonful of jam is allowed to go cold on a cold saucer and forms a wrinkled skin when a finger is pushed through.

If a good set is not reached, continue to cook for a further 2–5 minutes then re-test. To ensure that fruit does not float to the top of the jar, cool for 10 minutes before potting.

Seville Orange Marmalade

Softening the fruit in the Simmering Oven is the method that most Aga owners swear by – it is so much easier to cut up the fruit after the peel is cooked. Serve with some Aga Toast (see page 4) for a delicious homemade breakfast.

Yields 2.7kg (6 lb)
2kg (4 lb 8 oz) sugar
1kg (2 lb 2 oz) Seville
   oranges
juice of 3 lemons
1.8 litres (3¼ pints) water

PREPARE AHEAD
The marmalade will keep for up to 6 months in a cool place.

CONVENTIONAL OVEN
Cook on the hob in the usual way.

VARIATIONS
**MUSCOVADO DARK
SEVILLE MARMALADE**
Replace 225g (8 oz) sugar with 225g (8 oz) dark muscovado sugar.

GINGER MARMALADE
Add 225g (8 oz) chopped preserved ginger after the sugar has dissolved.

WHISKY MARMALADE
Add 8 tablespoons whisky to the marmalade just before potting.

1 Put the sugar to warm at the back of the Aga. Put the whole oranges and lemon juice in a large pan. Cover with the water. If it doesn't cover the oranges then use a smaller pan. If necessary, weight the oranges down with a Pyrex plate to keep them under the water. Bring the pan to the boil and cover.

2 Transfer the pan to the Simmering Oven and cook until tender – check after 2 hours. Remove the lid. Stand a colander on a deep plate, lift out the fruit and put into the colander. Allow to cool enough to handle. Leave the orange liquid in the pan for the time being. Cut the oranges in half. Scoop out all the pips and pith and add these to the orange liquid in the pan. Bring to the boil for 6 minutes with the lid off.

3 Strain this liquid through a sieve, pressing the pulp through with a wooden spoon. This thicker liquid is high in pectin and helps to give the marmalade a good set. Pour this liquid into a pan or preserving pan. At this stage the liquid should measure 1.3 litres (2¼ pints), reduce if necessary.

4 Cut up the peel with a sharp knife as thin as you like. Add the peel to the liquid in the large pan with the sugar. Stir on the Simmering Plate until the sugar has dissolved. Transfer to the Boiling Plate and boil rapidly for 8–10 minutes until setting point is reached (see page 9). Leave in the pan for 10 minutes to cool a little then pot, seal and label.

Strawberry Jam

Strawberries are particularly low in pectin and acid so a sugar containing these is a boon for quick reliable results.

Yields 2.7kg (6 lb)
1.3kg (3 lb) prepared
    strawberries,
    equivalent to 1.6kg
    (3½ lb) unprepared
    strawberries
1.3kg (3 lb) jam sugar
knob of butter

1 Check fruit, removing any over-ripe or bad strawberries. Place in a large pan. Crush with a potato masher or purée first in a processor. Add the sugar and heat gently on the Simmering Plate, stirring continuously until the sugar has dissolved.

2 Transfer to the Boiling Plate to bring to a fast rolling boil that will not stir down, for 4 minutes. Remove from the heat and stir in the butter. Ladle into warm jars and screw down the lids tightly as each jar is filled.

TIP
To reduce scum, add a knob of butter to the jam or marmalade before bringing to the full rolling boil.

PREPARE AHEAD
The jam will keep for up to 6 months.

CONVENTIONAL OVEN
Cook on the hob in the usual way.

Scotch Pancakes

These are simple to make and a great standby for unexpected guests.

100g (4 oz) self-raising
    flour
25g (1 oz) caster sugar
1 egg
150ml (¼ pint) milk
lard or oil, for greasing

1 Put the flour and sugar in a bowl, make a well in the centre and add the egg and half the milk. Beat to a thick batter. Stir in the remaining milk.

2 Grease the Simmering Plate lightly with lard or oil. Use a pad of kitchen paper for this. When ready to cook the pancakes, the fat should be just hazy – wipe off any surplus with more kitchen paper. If your Aga is particularly hot, it may be necessary to lift the lid of the Simmering Plate for a few minutes to reduce the heat before cooking.

3 Spoon the mixture on to the plate in tablespoonfuls, spacing them well apart. When bubbles rise to the surface, turn the pancakes over with a palette knife and cook on the other side for a further 30 seconds or so until golden brown. Lift off and keep warm and soft by wrapping in a clean tea towel. Continue cooking until all the batter has been used and then serve warm with butter and strawberry jam.

PREPARE AHEAD
The batter can be made up to 6 hours ahead.

CONVENTIONAL OVEN
Cook in a frying pan over a medium heat on the hob.

Buckwheat Pancakes

Simple to make and lovely to serve with butter and honey or cherry jam.

50g (2 oz) buckwheat
  flour
50g (2 oz) plain flour
2 level teaspoons
  baking powder
1 teaspoon runny honey
1 egg
150ml (¼ pint) milk
lard or oil, for greasing

1 Put the flours, baking powder and honey in a bowl, make a well in the centre and add the egg and half the milk. Beat to a thick batter. Stir in the remaining milk.

2 Grease the Simmering Plate lightly with lard or oil. (See page 12 for tips on how to do this.)

3 Spoon the mixture on to the plate in tablespoonfuls, spacing them well apart. When bubbles rise to the surface, turn the pancakes over with a palette knife and cook on the other side for a further 30 seconds or so until golden brown. Lift off and keep warm and soft by wrapping in a clean tea towel. Continue cooking until all the batter has been used and then serve warm.

Shrove Tuesday Pancakes

A classic for Pancake Day. Mary's grandchildren like their pancakes with ice cream and chocolate sauce.

100g (4 oz) plain flour
2 eggs
250ml (9 fl oz) milk
butter or oil, for
  greasing
lemon and sugar,
  to serve

1 Measure the flour into a bowl and make a well in the centre. Crack in the eggs and whisk by hand, pouring in the milk until smooth.

2 Heat a small 20cm (8 in) frying pan on the Boiling Plate. Melt a knob of butter or oil to grease the pan and then pour in the batter to give a thin coating. Once the edges start to curl and bubbles appear, toss the pancake to cook the other side.

3 Serve with lemon juice and caster sugar.

Lancashire Cheese and Rocket Tart

Made in the small roasting tin – for a party, double the ingredients and make in the large roasting tin. The cooking time will be a little longer and it will serve 16. No need to bake the pastry blind when cooking on the floor of the Roasting Oven – the intense heat on the floor will cook the pastry.

175g (6 oz) plain flour
75g (3 oz) butter, chilled
  and cut into cubes
7 eggs
1 tablespoon sunflower oil
1 large onion, chopped
100g (4 oz) fresh rocket,
  thick stems removed
  and roughly chopped
300ml (½ pint) double cream
300ml (½ pint) milk
salt and freshly ground
  black pepper
1 teaspoon Dijon mustard
100g (4 oz) Lancashire
  cheese, grated
75g (3 oz) Cheddar
  cheese, grated

PREPARE AHEAD

Can be made completely up to 2 days ahead and reheated in the Roasting Oven for 15 minutes to serve. Freezes well.

CONVENTIONAL OVEN

Bake the pastry blind in an oven preheated to 200°C/Fan 180°C/Gas 6 for 15 minutes. Cook the tart for about 25–35 minutes, turning after 15 minutes, until the pastry is pale golden brown and the filling is just set and golden all over.

1 For the pastry, measure the flour and butter into a mixer and whiz until the mixture resembles fine breadcrumbs. Add one of the eggs and whiz again to form a dough. Knead lightly and roll out on a lightly floured surface. Use to line the base and sides of the small roasting tin. Trim then flute the top edge and chill in the fridge.

2 Measure the oil into a pan on the Boiling Plate. Add the onion and fry for a few minutes, cover and transfer to the Simmering Oven to cook for about 20 minutes, until pale golden.

3 Meanwhile whisk the remaining 6 eggs in a large bowl and then add the cream, milk, seasoning and mustard.

4 Remove the onion from the oven and return to the Boiling Plate for a couple of minutes to drive off any liquid. Add the rocket and fry for a minute until just wilted. Spoon over the base of the pastry. Pour over the egg mixture and sprinkle with the cheeses.

5 If you have an Aga Total Control or City60, remove the floor grid in the Roasting Oven before baking. Cook on the floor of the Roasting Oven for about 25–35 minutes, turning after 15 minutes, until the pastry is pale golden brown and the filling is just set and golden all over. Don't be tempted to cook for too long as the filling will puff up and overcook.

Toasted Sandwiches

If making lots of sandwiches, it is best to use the Roasting Oven (see recipe below). For one or two sandwiches, cook on a piece of silicone paper on the Simmering Plate (see photo opposite and follow the method on page 21).

rashers streaky bacon
slices of brown
  or white bread
butter
cheese, cut into slices

PREPARE AHEAD
The sandwiches can be made up to 2 hours ahead and cooked to serve.

CONVENTIONAL OVEN
Cook under a hot grill in the usual way.

1 Begin by cooking the streaky bacon in the Aga roasting tin at the top of the Roasting Oven until crisp.

2 Meanwhile, butter one side of each slice of bread. Place the bacon on one unbuttered piece, top with as much cheese as you like and then place a second slice of bread, buttered side up, on top. Place on a baking sheet, butter side down. Keep repeating this process until you have the number of sandwiches you need.

3 If you have an Aga Total Control or City60, remove the floor grid in the Roasting Oven before baking. Slide the baking sheet on to the floor of the Roasting Oven for about 10 minutes, turning the sandwiches over after 5 minutes until nicely browned and crisp. For French stick toasties, split the bread and prepare as open sandwiches.

VARIATIONS

TUNA MAYONNAISE
1 × 198g (7 oz) tin of tuna fish
1½ tablespoons mayonnaise
freshly ground black pepper

Combine the tuna with the mayonnaise, season with pepper and pile on to the bread before toasting as above.

HAM AND MUSHROOM
slices of ham
mushrooms, thickly sliced
  and cooked in butter

Place a slice of ham on the bread and sprinkle over some cooked mushrooms before toasting as above.

CHEESE, TOMATO AND AVOCADO
slices of Cheddar cheese
  and Brie
slices of firm tomato
avocado mashed with
  lemon juice

Place the cheeses, tomato and avocado on the bread, sandwich together and then toast as above.

Quesadillas

Great for brunch or a snack for growing teenagers! Choose fillings of your choice and vary the type of cheese. Lowering the lid after turning the quesadillas will help the filling melt.

1 ripe avocado, peeled
    and cut into small dice
1 firm tomato, deseeded
    and diced
¼ red chilli, finely diced
1 heaped tablespoon
    mango chutney
100g (4 oz) mature
    Cheddar cheese
a squeeze of lemon
salt and freshly
    ground pepper
2 large flour tortilla
    wraps

1 Measure the avocado, tomato, chilli, chutney, cheese and lemon into a bowl, season with salt and pepper and mix well to combine.

2 Lay a piece of silicone paper on the work surface and sit one tortilla on top. Spoon the avocado mixture on top and spread to the edges. Sit the other tortilla on top and press down slightly so they stick.

3 Lift the lid of the Simmering Plate, slide the silicone paper on top and cook the underside of the wrap for a few minutes. Once toasted turn over carefully, lower the lid and cook for a further 3 minutes or until the filling is just melted and the wrap is golden.

4 Slide on to a board and cut into wedges to serve.

PREPARE AHEAD
The filling can be made 6 hours ahead and kept in the fridge.

CONVENTIONAL OVEN
Cook in a frying pan over a high heat.

Pizza

This recipe is for two large pizzas – it always seems sensible to us to make one to eat now and one for the freezer. Of course you can make your own dough but, as this is for brunch or a snack, it is quicker to buy the mix and there are very good products available nowadays.

1 packet white
    bread mix
handful of chopped
    fresh basil and parsley
125g (4½ oz) mozzarella
    cheese, sliced
12 black olives, pitted
handful of rocket,
    to serve
shavings of Parmesan
    cheese, to serve

TOMATO BASE

2 tablespoons olive oil
2 large onions, chopped
2 fat garlic cloves,
    crushed
600ml (1 pint) passata
225g (8 oz) tomato
    purée
salt and freshly ground
    black pepper

PREPARE AHEAD
Pizza can be made a few hours
ahead and cooked to serve.

CONVENTIONAL OVEN
Preheat a baking sheet to
get very hot and then cook
the pizza on it in an oven
preheated to 200°C/Fan
180°C/Gas 6 for 20 minutes.

1 Mix the dough base according to the packet instructions. Cover and leave near the Aga until doubled in size, for about 30 minutes.

2 Meanwhile to make the tomato base, heat the oil in a large pan on the Boiling Plate, add the onions and garlic and fry for a minute. Cover with a lid and transfer to the Simmering Oven for about 10 minutes until soft.

3 Return to the Boiling Plate, add the passata and the purée and season with salt and pepper. Boil for 4–5 minutes to thicken. Set aside to cool.

4 Divide the dough in half and roll out two circles about 25cm (10 in) in diameter. Lift on to lightly greased baking trays. Spread the tomato mixture on to the bases and sprinkle with the chopped fresh herbs.

5 Layer the pizza bases with slices of mozzarella cheese and scatter over the olives.

6 Cook on the floor of the Roasting Oven for 15 minutes, then with the grid shelf on the highest set of runners, transfer to the top of the oven for a further 5–10 minutes, until the dough is golden and risen.

7 To serve, pile the rocket in the centre of the pizza and shave over some Parmesan.

VARIATION
Arrange 3 slices of Parma ham on top, if liked.

STARTERS

STOCKPOT

One of the great joys of an Aga is always having stock on hand as it freezes well. Use the largest Aga pan you have with a well-fitting lid. Make your stockpot overnight in the Simmering Oven – the gentle, controlled heat will extract all the goodness from the bones. After straining off the stock, the bones can be thrown away.

The best bones to use are beef, veal, poultry and game, including all the giblets. You can use non-fatty pork, lamb and mutton bones for broth. Don't include the following in stock: starchy vegetables, mixed raw and cooked bones (use for separate stocks), extra fat, or cooked green vegetables – they become overcooked, especially cabbage and sprouts.

Meat stocks keep for up to 1 week in the fridge or 3 months in the freezer.

VEGETABLE STOCK

selection of vegetables, i.e. root
  vegetables (though not too many
  strongly flavoured ones like swede,
  parsnip, carrot and leeks) and the
  outer leaves of green vegetables (only
  to be added for the last 20 minutes)
salt and freshly ground black pepper

1 Roughly chop the vegetables, add water to cover, season and bring to the boil. Simmer for 5 minutes then cover with a lid.

2 Transfer to the floor of the Simmering Oven for about 3 hours. Strain and use. This is good for sauces to accompany vegetables. Remember vegetable stock does not keep well. Use within 3 days.

GOOD BEEF STOCK

as many sawn beef marrow bones
  as you can fit into your largest pan
2 onions, quartered
1 carrot
2 sticks of celery
sprig of thyme, bay leaf
  and a few parsley stalks
salt and black pepper

1 Put the bones into the large Aga roasting tin and cook in the Roasting Oven for about 45 minutes to brown the bones.

2 Lift out of the oven and transfer to your largest pan. Add the remaining ingredients, add water to cover, bring to the boil and simmer for 10 minutes.

3 Cover with a lid and transfer to the floor of the Simmering Oven overnight.

4 The next morning, skim off any fat and strain.

LIGHT STOCK

chicken, turkey or veal bones
2 onions, quartered
1 carrot
2 sticks of celery
sprig of thyme, bay leaf
and a few parsley stalks
salt and black pepper

1 Place all the ingredients in a large
saucepan, add water to cover, bring
to the boil and simmer for 10 minutes.

2 Cover with a lid and transfer to the
floor of the Simmering Oven overnight.

3 The next morning, skim off any
fat and strain.

GAME STOCK

carcass of game birds,
including giblets
2 onions, quartered
2 sticks of celery
sprig of thyme, bay leaf
and a few parsley stalks
salt and black pepper

1 Place all the ingredients in a large
saucepan, add water to cover, bring
to the boil and simmer for 10 minutes.

2 Cover with a lid and transfer to the
floor of the Simmering Oven overnight.

3 The next morning, skim off any fat
and strain.

FAMILY STOCK

leftover joint bones or chicken
carcasses, cooked
leftover root vegetables
salt and freshly ground black pepper

1 Place all the ingredients in a large
saucepan, add water to cover, bring
to the boil and simmer for 10 minutes.

2 Cover with a lid and transfer to the
floor of the Simmering Oven for 2 hours.

3 Skim off any fat and strain.

FISH STOCK

450g (1 lb) white fish bones and
trimmings (avoid strong oily fish)
1 onion, peeled and quartered
1 stick of celery
salt and freshly ground black pepper

1 Wash the bones and trimmings
and place in a large saucepan.

2 Add the other ingredients, add water
to cover, bring to the boil and skim.
Bring to the boil again. Cover.

3 Transfer to the floor of the Simmering
Oven for 1 hour. Strain. Cool and store
covered in the fridge for up to 3 days.

French Onion Soup

Always a favourite and so simple to make.
The kick of sherry is what makes it special.

50g (2 oz) butter
1 tablespoon
    sunflower oil
3 large onions,
    very finely sliced
1 tablespoon
    brown sugar
3 tablespoons
    plain flour
100ml (3½ fl oz) sherry
1.5 litres (2½ pints)
    good chicken
    or beef stock, hot
salt and freshly
    ground black pepper

TO SERVE
12 slices of thin
    French bread
a little Dijon mustard
50g (2 oz) Gruyère
    cheese, grated

1 Heat the butter and oil in a deep saucepan on the Boiling Plate. Add the onions and fry for 2 minutes. Cover with a lid and transfer to the Simmering Oven for about 20 minutes or until soft.

2 Return to the Boiling Plate, add the sugar and fry for a minute, stirring quickly, until golden brown. Remove from the heat and sprinkle in the flour. Stir, return to the heat and blend in the sherry and stock. Season, cover with a lid and transfer to the Simmering Oven for about 10 minutes.

3 Meanwhile, toast the bread on one side on the Simmering Plate. Spread the untoasted side with a little mustard and then sprinkle with the cheese Arrange the croûtes on a baking tray and slide on to the top set of runners in the Roasting Oven for about 4 minutes, or until the cheese is melted.

4 Pour the piping hot soup into bowls and place 2 toasted croûtes on each serving.

PREPARE AHEAD
The soup can be completed to the end of step 2, quickly cooled, then stored in a sealed container in the fridge for up to 2 days. It also freezes well for up to 1 month.

CONVENTIONAL OVEN
Cook on the hob in the usual way.

Watercress and Celeriac Soup

Celeriac is a late summer and winter vegetable. You have to
peel it fairly thickly as it is such a knobbly shape. You might need
to pop it in a little acidulated water (water with lemon juice)
to prevent it discolouring after peeling.

2 bunches of watercress
65g (2½ oz) butter
1 large onion, sliced
350g (12 oz) celeriac,
   peeled weight, cubed
40g (1½ oz) plain flour
1.2 litres (2 pints)
   chicken stock
salt and freshly ground
   black pepper
about 300ml (½ pint)
   milk, boiling
a little single cream

1 Wash the watercress but do not remove the stalks.
Trim off a small bunch of leaves to use for garnish
if not freezing.

2 Melt the butter in a saucepan on the Boiling Plate
and gently toss the onion and celeriac, not letting them
brown. Add the flour, mix well, then add the stock
and seasoning. Bring to the boil, then simmer, covered,
for 5 minutes on the Simmering Plate. Transfer to the
floor of the Simmering Oven, covered, for 30 minutes
until tender.

3 Add the watercress, with stalks, and simmer for
a further 5 minutes on the Simmering Plate. Purée
the soup in a processor or liquidiser, return the soup
to the pan and add the boiling milk to make the
required consistency. Check seasoning.

4 To serve, stir in a little cream and sprinkle each
serving with the reserved finely chopped watercress
leaves. Do not keep the soup hot for any length
of time, as it will go grey in colour.

PREPARE AHEAD
The soup can be completed
to the end of step 3, quickly
cooled, then stored in a sealed
container in the fridge for up
to 2 days. It also freezes well
for up to 1 month.

CONVENTIONAL OVEN
Cook on the hob in the usual way.

Soup à la Reine

This is a superb soup and no one would guess
it was based on the humble parsnip.

50g (2 oz) butter
1 tablespoon
    sunflower oil
450g (1 lb) parsnips,
    cubed
1 fat garlic clove,
    crushed
1 onion, chopped
25g (1 oz) flour
1 rounded teaspoon
    curry powder
1.2 litres (2 pints)
    good stock
salt and freshly ground
    black pepper

TO GARNISH
150ml (¼ pint)
    single cream
a few snipped chives

1 Heat the butter and oil in a deep pan and add
the parsnips, garlic and onion and fry gently
on the Simmering Plate for about 10 minutes.

2 Stir in the flour and curry powder and cook for
a minute, then slowly stir in the stock, season and
bring to the boil. Cover and simmer for 5 minutes.

3 Transfer to the floor of the Simmering Oven
and leave to cook for about 40 minutes or until
the parsnips are tender.

4 Purée the soup in a processor or blender then
return to the pan. Bring back up to a simmer
and taste to check seasoning.

5 Serve with a swirl of cream and a few snipped
chives sprinkled on top.

PREPARE AHEAD
The soup can be prepared up
to the end of step 4, quickly
cooled, then stored in a sealed
container in the fridge for up
to 2 days. It also freezes well
for up to 1 month.

CONVENTIONAL OVEN
Cook on the hob in the usual way.

Chèvre and Tomato Bruschetta

These are also good served with drinks – a narrow French
stick can be cut into 20–28 pieces. Red pesto makes
a lovely alternative to sun-dried tomato paste.

½ large French stick
butter, for spreading
about 3 tablespoons
   sun-dried tomato paste
1 tablespoon chopped
   fresh basil
about 225–275g
   (8–10 oz) goat's cheese
paprika

1 Slice the French stick into 5mm (¼ in) rounds and
butter both sides. Arrange on baking parchment on
a baking sheet.

2 Spread a little of the sun-dried tomato paste on
to one side of the bread and sprinkle with a little
chopped basil.

3 Slice the goats' cheese very thinly and arrange
on top of the tomato paste. Dust lightly with a
little paprika.

4 Bake on the floor of the Roasting Oven for about
8–10 minutes, watching carefully, until melted and
golden brown. Serve on dressed salad leaves.

TIP

If you need something to
brown quickly - toasted
savouries to have with drinks,
or vegetables - sprinkly a little
paprika on top before you pop it
in the top of the oven. It adds to
the taste, too!

PREPARE AHEAD

Can be made a day ahead.
Freezes well uncooked.

CONVENTIONAL OVEN

Bake in an oven preheated
to 220°C/Fan 200°C/Gas 7
for about 8–10 minutes or
until the cheese is melted
and golden brown. Or grill.

Oven-baked Aga Croûtons

2 slices of white bread
2 tablespoons olive oil
salt and freshly ground
   black pepper

PREPARE AHEAD
The croûtons can be
made a few hours ahead.

CONVENTIONAL OVEN
Fry over a medium heat
until golden brown.

1 Remove the crusts from the bread and cut into 1cm
(½ in) cubes. Measure the oil into a large polythene
bag and add the bread. Shake to coat evenly, season
well and spread out into the small roasting tin.

2 Place the tin on the floor of the Roasting Oven
and cook for about 6 minutes until golden brown.
Keep turning the cubes at intervals to prevent
them browning too quickly.

3 Drain on kitchen paper and serve.

Melba Toast

6 slices of white bread

PREPARE AHEAD
Once cool, the toast can be
stored in an airtight tin for
2 days. If necessary re-crisp
in the Roasting Oven for 2
minutes before serving.

CONVENTIONAL OVEN
Toast the bread and cut as
above. Place the triangles in a
roasting tin and bake in an oven
preheated to 200°C/Fan 180°C/
Gas 6 for about 10 minutes.

1 Toast the slices of bread in the Aga Toaster
on the Boiling Plate (see page 4).

2 Remove the crusts with a sharp knife and then cut
the bread in half horizontally through the doughy
middle. Cut each slice in half diagonally to create
two triangles. Put the slices of toast in a roasting tin.

3 Hang the tin on the lowest set of runners in the
Roasting Oven for 8–10 minutes and allow the bread
to toast to a pale golden brown and the edges to curl.
Do watch to check they don't overbrown.

4 Leave to cool on a wire rack before serving.

Garlic Bread

A large French stick needs more butter.

1 French stick
2 fat garlic cloves,
    crushed
salt and freshly ground
    black pepper
1 tablespoon very
    finely chopped flat-
    leaf parsley
about 75g (3 oz) butter

1 Lay a large piece of foil on a work surface. Make wide diagonal cuts through the bread.

2 Beat the garlic, seasoning and parsley into the butter until soft and smooth. Spread the garlic butter on each side of the bread slices and ease it back into its original shape on the foil. Spread any remaining butter over the crust. Bring the foil up round the bread leaving the top open to allow it to brown.

3 Slide on to the highest set of runners and cook in the Roasting Oven for about 6 minutes until golden and the butter has just melted.

PREPARE AHEAD
The bread can be prepared to the end of step 2 a day ahead. It can also be frozen wrapped in clingfilm for up to 1 month.

CONVENTIONAL OVEN
Bake in an oven preheated to 200°C/Fan 180°C/Gas 6 for about 6 minutes until golden and the butter has just melted.

Swiss Double Soufflés

This also makes a delicious lunch dish, served
with crusty bread and a mixed leaf salad.

SOUFFLÉ
butter, for greasing
100g (4 oz) leaf spinach
300ml (10 fl oz) milk
40g (1½ oz) butter
40g (1½ oz) plain flour
salt and freshly ground
    black pepper
¼ level teaspoon freshly
    grated nutmeg
50g (2 oz) Gruyère
    cheese, grated
3 eggs, separated

TOPPING
50g (2 oz) Parmesan
    cheese, grated
300ml (10 fl oz)
    double cream

1 Butter six small (9 × 4cm / 3½ × 1½ in) ramekin
dishes very generously. Wash the spinach and shred
it finely. Put the spinach in a saucepan with the milk
and bring to the boil on the Boiling Plate. Stir well
and set aside.

2 Melt the butter in a generous-sized saucepan on
the Simmering Plate, remove the pan from the heat
and blend in the flour. Return to the heat, whisk and
cook the roux for 1 minute, stirring all the time.

3 Add the spinach and milk a little at a time and bring
to the boil, stirring constantly. Simmer until the sauce
is thick and smooth.

4 Remove the pan from the heat and beat in the salt,
pepper, nutmeg and Gruyère cheese. When these
are well incorporated, stir in the egg yolks.

5 Whisk the egg whites until stiff and fold carefully
into the sauce mixture.

6 Spoon the mixture into the prepared dishes and
place them in a small roasting tin. Pour boiling water
into the tin to come halfway up the dishes. Cook
in the bain-marie in the Roasting Oven on the grid
shelf on the floor for 15–20 minutes. After 10 minutes,
or when the soufflés are a perfect golden brown, turn
round if necessary, and slide in the cold plain shelf
on the second set of runners. Continue cooking until
they are springy to the touch. Leave for 5–10 minutes
in the ramekin dishes to shrink back.

PREPARE AHEAD
Complete to step 8 up to
2 days ahead. It is possible
to freeze the wrapped, cooked
soufflés for up to 1 month.
Reheat as step 9.

CONVENTIONAL OVEN
Cook in an oven preheated to
220°C/Fan 200°C/Gas 7 for
15–20 minutes until golden
and springy to the touch.
Leave to stand for 5–10
minutes, then continue with
steps 7–9, returning to the
oven for 15–20 minutes,
until golden.

7 Butter a shallow gratin dish, which is large enough
to hold the little soufflés without them touching each
other. Sprinkle half the Parmesan on the bottom of
the dish.

8 Run the blade of a small palette knife round the edges
of the little soufflés, then unmould them carefully and
put them into the gratin dish.

9 Season the cream and pour over the little soufflés.
Sprinkle the rest of the Parmesan over the surface,
and bake in the Roasting Oven as before, but without
the cold plain shelf, for another 15–20 minutes or until
the soufflés have puffed up and are golden.

VARIATIONS
Choose any flavouring and add to the mixture
before the egg yolks.

SMOKED HAM
Add 100g (4 oz) finely chopped fried Parma ham.

FISH
Add 100g (4 oz) finely chopped smoked salmon.

SHELLFISH
Add 100g (4 oz) peeled cooked prawns or shrimps.

MUSHROOM
Add 175g (6 oz) finely chopped sautéed mushrooms.

Spinach and Feta Samosas

These quantities will make 24 samosas – you can either serve four
per person as a starter, or use them as a pre-dinner nibble.

about 10 sheets filo
pastry (about 15 ×
30cm/6 ×12 in)
about 50g (2 oz) butter,
melted, for brushing

FILLING

50g (2 oz) butter
100g (4 oz) baby
spinach
50g (2 oz) feta cheese,
crumbled
50g (2 oz) full-fat cream
cheese
2 teaspoons Dijon
mustard
salt and freshly ground
black pepper
little grated nutmeg

1 To make the filling, melt the butter in a pan, add the
spinach and fry on the Boiling Plate until just wilted.
Drain in a colander and press to squeeze out all the
liquid. Tip into a bowl, add the cheeses and mustard
and season with salt, pepper and nutmeg.

2 Lay the filo pastry out on a board or work surface one
sheet at a time, keeping the rest covered with a damp
cloth to prevent it drying out and becoming brittle.
Cut the pastry into strips about 5 × 25cm (2 × 10 in).
Brush each pastry strip with melted butter.

3 Put a teaspoonful of the spinach mixture on to the
bottom corner of each strip of pastry. Fold the pastry
over so that it forms a triangle, then continue folding
the triangle over itself until you reach the end of the
strip. Arrange on baking parchment on a baking sheet.

4 Continue with more strips of filo pastry until all the
filling is used up. Brush the tops of each samosa with
melted butter.

5 Bake on the grid shelf on the floor of the Roasting
Oven for about 10 minutes, then put directly on to the
floor of the Roasting Oven to brown the bases – about
a further 5 minutes. Serve immediately.

PREPARE AHEAD
Prepare to the end of step 4.
Cover and keep in the fridge for
up to a day ahead. The unbaked
samosas can be packed and
frozen for up to 1 month.

CONVENTIONAL OVEN
Bake in an oven preheated to
200°C/Fan 180°C/Gas 6 for
about 15 minutes or until the
pastry is crisp and golden.

VARIATION

LEEK, GOAT'S CHEESE AND SUN-DRIED TOMATO SAMOSAS

25g (1 oz) butter
1 small leek (about 100g/4 oz), washed and finely sliced
50g (2 oz) crumbly goat's cheese, such as chèvre, in a roll
25g (1 oz) sun-dried tomatoes, drained from their oil
   and snipped into small pieces
salt and freshly ground black pepper

1 Melt the butter in a small pan and add the leek. Cook gently on the Simmering Plate until soft with a hint of colour. Allow to cool. Gently stir in the cheese and sun-dried tomatoes and season to taste.

2 Mix together and use to fill the samosas as above.

Hot-smoked Salmon and Dill Pâté

Quick, tasty and perfect to be made ahead and served with Melba Toast (see page 34). Hot-smoked salmon is cooked smoked rather than dry smoked and the combination of the two makes a moist pâté. You can serve in individual ramekins, as Mary does, or in one big bowl for everyone to dig in, like Lucy.

50g (2 oz) butter
juice of 1 small lemon
2 tablespoons capers
100g (4 oz) hot-smoked
    salmon flakes
100g (4 oz) smoked
    salmon
1 small bunch of
    dill, torn into
    smaller pieces
1 × 180g (6 oz) tub of
    full-fat cream cheese
freshly ground black
    pepper

TO GARNISH
6 sprigs of fresh dill
1 tablespoon capers
wedge of lemon

1 You will need 6 small ramekins or china pots, or an open sharing bowl.

2 Measure the butter, lemon juice and capers into a small pan, heat on the Simmering Plate of the Aga and stir until melted. Set aside to cool for about 5 minutes.

3 Measure both the smoked salmons into a processor, add the dill and whiz until roughly chopped. Pour in the melted butter mixture and whiz again for 5 seconds. Add the cream cheese and pepper and whiz again until just combined (still with texture, not a purée). Spoon into the ramekins or sharing bowl and leave to chill for about an hour.

4 To serve, bring to room temperature and garnish with fresh dill, a few capers and a wedge lemon.

PREPARE AHEAD
Can be made up to 2 days ahead.

CONVENTIONAL OVEN
Cook on the hob in the usual way.

Bacon and Gruyère Tartlets

These are great for a starter or light lunch. Vary the filling
as you wish but keep the liquid filling and cheese the same.

PASTRY

175g (6 oz) plain flour
2 teaspoons dried
  mustard powder
100g (4 oz) butter,
  cubed
1 egg, beaten

FILLING

a knob of butter
1 onion, thinly sliced
250g (9 oz) streaky
  bacon, chopped
2 eggs, beaten
200ml (⅓ pint)
  double cream
salt and freshly
  ground black pepper
3 tablespoons chopped
  fresh parsley
100g (4 oz) Gruyère
  cheese, grated

1 You will need 2 × 4-hole Yorkshire pudding tins.

2 To make the pastry, measure the flour, mustard
powder and butter into a processor and whiz until like
breadcrumbs. Add the egg and whiz again to form a ball.

3 Roll the dough out thinly on a floured work surface,
cut into eight circles and use them to line the Yorkshire
pudding tins.

4 To make the filling, melt the butter in a frying pan
on the Boiling Plate, add the onion and bacon and fry
for a few minutes. Cover and transfer to the Simmering
Oven for about 10–15 minutes until soft and cooked.
Return to the Boiling Plate, drive off any liquid and
set aside to cool a little.

5 Measure the eggs and cream into a jug and beat
with a hand whisk. Season with salt and pepper.

6 Add some of the bacon and onion mixture to each
pastry circle. Sprinkle with the fresh parsley and
pour over the egg mixture. Top with the cheese.

7 Bake on the grid shelf on the floor of the Roasting
Oven for about 15 minutes, until golden on top and
the pastry is crisp. If the tarts start to get too brown,
slide the cold sheet on to the second set of runners.

8 Serve hot or warm with some green salad leaves.

PREPARE AHEAD
Can be made a day ahead and
reheated in the Simmering
Oven to serve. They also
freeze well cooked.

CONVENTIONAL OVEN
Slide the tins on to a preheated
baking sheet and cook in an
oven preheated to 200°C/Fan
180°C/Gas 6 for 15 minutes.

MAIN
COURSES

WAYS OF COOKING FISH

Rich in protein, low in fat and carbohydrate, it's little wonder that fish is becoming more and more popular. Remember, fish takes very little cooking, so do note that it is rarely necessary to pre-poach fish before cooking in pastry or baking in a sauce. Overcooked fish becomes dry, stringy and flavourless. Take advantage, too, of the seasonality of fish and ring the changes according to the availability and peak perfection of different varieties.

POACHING

SALMON

USING A FISH KETTLE

Half fill with boiling water, add 2 tablespoons salt, 3 bay leaves, 1 sliced onion, 12 peppercorns and 1 lemon cut into wedges. Bring to the boil on the Boiling Plate and then put in the fish.

under 2.2kg (5 lb) return to the boil for 2 minutes and then remove from the heat
2.2–3.2kg (5–7 lb) return to the boil, simmer for 3 minutes and then remove from the heat
3.2–4.5kg (7–10 lb) return to the boil, simmer for 4 minutes and then remove from the heat

Leave the lid on and the fish inside until it is lukewarm, then lift out and remove the skin. It is easier to remove the skin when warm, rather than cold.

ROASTING OVEN METHOD

Remove the head, season and wrap in buttered foil. Place in the large roasting tin. Pour boiling water around the fish to come halfway up the tin. Slide on to the lowest set of runners in the Roasting Oven. Turn the fish over halfway through.

1kg (2¼ lb) about 10 minutes
1.3kg (3 lb) about 15 minutes
1.8kg (4 lb) about 20 minutes
2.7kg (6 lb) about 25 minutes
3.6kg (8 lb) about 30 minutes
4.5kg (10 lb) about 35 minutes
5.4kg (12 lb) about 40 minutes

Leave the salmon in the foil to become lukewarm, then skin and garnish.
To serve the fish hot, increase cooking time by one-third and leave in the hot water for 15 minutes before serving.

COD, BREAM, HADDOCK, HALIBUT, MONK FISH AND TROUT

Put the fish in 600ml (1 pint) cold water in a pan and add ½ tablespoon salt, 1 bay leaf and ½ a lemon cut into wedges. Bring to the boil on the Boiling Plate then simmer gently for 2 minutes. Cover and transfer to the Simmering Oven. Allow 10 minutes per 450g (1 lb) and 10 minutes over. Drain thoroughly.

FILLETS

You can oven steam, pan or oven fry, or roast fillets of fish, depending on personal choice. Hake and smoked fish fillets are great for steaming and monk fish and trout roast very well. We enjoy fried plaice, haddock and cod.

OVEN STEAMING

Take a buttered ovenproof dish, arrange the fish in a single layer – or roll up the fillets. Season, add butter and a little milk or fish stock, parsley stalks, a bay leaf and some peppercorns. Cover. Cook in the Roasting Oven for 5 minutes then transfer to the Simmering Oven for about 20 minutes or more until the fish is opaque and cooked through. Use the strained fish juices and stock for a sauce.

PAN FRYING

It is easy to pan fry fillets. Choose all the same-sized fresh fillets with skin on. Heat a pan on the Boiling Plate. Brush both sides of the fish fillets with oil. Fry top side down for about 1 minute, carefully turn over so the skin is on the bottom, transfer to the floor of the Roasting Oven and continue to cook for about 4–5 minutes (depending on the thickness of the fillet) until the skin is crispy and cooked through.

OVEN FRYING

We prefer to fry in a little sunflower oil in the Roasting Oven – no smells! We do not deep-fat fry so do not use batter. Dry the fish after washing and coat with either: seasoned flour, fine oatmeal for herrings and mackerel, egg and fresh white breadcrumbs or panko breadcrumbs. Polenta and semolina give a nice coating, too. Use just enough oil to cover the base of the Aga roasting tin. Preheat on the floor of the Roasting Oven until smoking, then cook the fish in the roasting tin on the floor of the oven. Start with the white side down and then turn the fish halfway through cooking so that the dark-skinned side is under for serving.

ROASTING

If we are serving cold salmon fillets we line a large roasting tin with foil, season it with salt and pepper and then lay the skinned salmon fillets on top. Season the salmon and then dot with a little butter. Add a squeeze of lemon and lay another piece of foil on top, sealing the edges. Slide into the Simmering Oven for about 30 minutes or until just cooked. This is a very gentle way of cooking the fillets and perfect for serving with a herb sauce for a summer lunch or buffet.

SAUCES TO GO WITH FISH
ALL SAUCES SERVE 4

HOLLANDAISE SAUCE
MAKES 300ML (½ PINT)

If you have a large processor it is a good idea to tilt the machine so that the mixture gathers on one side. No need to tilt it in a blender or small processor. If you have no unsalted butter, use salted and discard the last runny, watery bit in the pan at the end. Hollandaise can be varied in a number of ways, see below.

6 tablespoons white wine vinegar
6 black peppercorns
bay leaf
225g (8 oz) unsalted butter
4 egg yolks
salt and freshly ground black pepper

1 Put the vinegar, peppercorns and bay leaf into a small pan and reduce on the Boiling Plate to about 1 tablespoon.

2 Melt the butter until boiling in another small pan on the same plate.

3 Thoroughly preheat the processor blade and bowl by pouring boiling water in, and then discarding the water. Add the egg yolks and strain in the warm vinegar. At once, turn on the food processor and, with the machine running, slowly trickle in the boiling, melted butter by pouring through the funnel. When all the butter has been added, season carefully. It should be lightly piquant, barely holding its shape, and lukewarm rather than hot.

PREPARE AHEAD
Make an hour ahead and keep warm on the back of the Aga, standing on a tea towel in the serving dish, or transfer to a heated wide-necked thermos flask to keep warm for up to 4 hours.

CONVENTIONAL OVEN
Reduce the vinegar and melt the butter on the hob in the usual way.

TIP
If you don't have a processor, measure the vinegar into a bowl and add the egg yolks. Whisk with a wire balloon whisk until well mixed. Place the bowl over a pan of hot water and whisk. Gradually add the just warm, not melted, butter, whisking after each addition until the sauce thickens and all the butter has been used. Season carefully and then serve.

VARIATIONS
BÉARNAISE SAUCE
This is Hollandaise sauce with added fresh herbs to serve with fish or meat. Add 1 tablespoon each chopped fresh thyme, parsley and marjoram. All herbs must be fresh.

DILL OR TARRAGON SAUCE
For fish. Add 2 tablespoons chopped fresh dill or 1 tablespoon chopped fresh tarragon.

CHIVE SAUCE
For meat, fish or eggs. Add 2 tablespoons chopped fresh chives.

MUSTARD OR HORSERADISH SAUCE
For beef. Add 2 tablespoons Dijon mustard or 2 tablespoons strong horseradish.

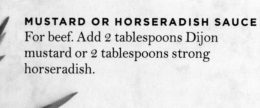

FRESH HERB SAUCE

75g (3 oz) butter, melted
juice of 1 lemon
1 rounded teaspoon flour
300ml (½ pint) single cream
1 egg yolk
salt and freshly ground black pepper
1 tablespoon chopped fresh dill or chives

1 Measure all the ingredients, except
the dill or chives, into a processor or
blender and blend until smooth.

2 Transfer to a bowl and stand over
a pan of simmering water for about
10 minutes, stirring from time to time,
until thickened. Season to taste and
stir in the dill or chives, transfer to
a serving dish and serve hot.

CUCUMBER AND DILL SAUCE

½ cucumber, diced
2 teaspoons salt
150ml (¼ pint) mayonnaise
150ml (¼ pint) whipping cream, whipped
juice of ½ a lemon
salt and freshly ground black pepper
2 tablespoons freshly snipped dill

1 Put the diced cucumber on to a plate
and sprinkle with the salt. Leave to stand
for 30 minutes, then rinse thoroughly
and drain well on kitchen paper.

2 Blend the mayonnaise and cream
together then gently stir in the lemon
juice, seasoning, cucumber and dill.
Turn into a serving bowl and serve
well chilled with salmon or trout.

THAI SAUCE

1 × 2.5cm (1 in) piece of fresh
  root ginger, peeled and cut
  into needle-thin strips
1 tablespoon olive oil
1 small garlic clove, crushed
1 small orange
1 scant teaspoon red Thai curry paste
300ml (½ pint) full-fat crème fraîche
salt and freshly ground black pepper

1 Soften the ginger in the oil in a
large-based pan on the Simmering
Plate for a minute, then add the garlic.
Stir well, cover, and transfer to the floor
of the Simmering Oven for 10 minutes.
(The reason for using a large pan is that
it is quicker to reduce the sauce later.)

2 Remove the rind from the orange
using a zester, then squeeze the juice.

3 Add the Thai paste to the ginger
and garlic mixture, stir well and then
add the orange juice and zest and the
crème fraîche. Bring to the boil on the
Boiling Plate, simmer for 2–3 minutes,
and season to taste. If necessary,
boil further to reduce to a creamy
consistency. Keep warm. Serve
with grilled fish, like salmon.

CREAMY DILL AND SHALLOT SAUCE

3 tablespoons whipping cream
½ small shallot
150ml (¼ pint) mayonnaise
juice of ½ a lemon
1 teaspoon freshly snipped dill
½ teaspoon each freshly chopped
   lemon thyme, parsley and chives
salt and freshly ground black pepper

1 Whip the cream and place in a basin.
Squeeze the shallot through a garlic
press and add to the cream with the rest
of the ingredients. Mix together until
blended. Taste and check seasoning.
Serve cold.

LIGHT HERB AIOLI

3 tablespoons chopped fresh parsley
3 tablespoons half-fat crème fraîche
3 tablespoons light mayonnaise
1 spring onion, chopped
1 tablespoon chopped fresh mint
1 tablespoon torn basil
½ garlic clove, crushed
juice of ½ a lime or lemon
salt and freshly ground black pepper

1 Simply mix all the ingredients
together and season well.

CHILLI ORIENTAL SAUCE

3 tablespoons soy sauce
2 tablespoons sesame,
   walnut or olive oil
½ teaspoon dried chilli flakes
1 tablespoon lime juice

1 Mix together to give a dressing
or sauce for poached fish.

LIME AND MUSTARD DRESSING

1 generous teaspoon
    coarse grain mustard
3 teaspoons caster sugar
juice of 2 limes
4 tablespoons olive oil
salt and freshly ground black pepper
2 tomatoes, skinned and seeded

1 Make the dressing by measuring
all the ingredients, except the
tomatoes, into a clean jam jar. Add salt
and pepper and give it a good shake.
Slice the skinned tomatoes into thin
strips and mix with the dressing.

TARTARE SAUCE

300ml (½ pint) mayonnaise
1 good tablespoon gherkins, chopped
1 good tablespoon capers, chopped
1 good tablespoon chopped
    fresh parsley
a squeeze of lemon juice
salt and freshly ground
    black pepper

1 Measure all the ingredients
into a bowl and mix well until
thoroughly blended. Turn into
a serving bowl and serve.

MUSTARD DILL SAUCE

1½ tablespoons Dijon mustard
1 tablespoon golden caster sugar
½ tablespoon white wine vinegar
1 small egg yolk
3 tablespoons sunflower oil
salt and freshly ground black pepper
1 tablespoon chopped fresh dill
    or ½ tablespoon dried dill

1 Whisk the mustard, sugar, vinegar
and egg yolk together in a bowl (a little
balloon whisk is ideal). Incorporate the
oil, whisking well. The result will be the
consistency of mayonnaise. Season with
salt and pepper and stir in the dill.

Salmon en Croûte with Asparagus

Full of flavour, colour and design.

700g (1 lb 9 oz) thick
    asparagus spears,
    trimmed
1 × 280g (10 oz) packet
    full-fat cream cheese
1 egg yolk
finely grated zest and
    juice of 1 lemon
1 good tablespoon
    chopped fresh parsley
1 good tablespoon
    chopped fresh
    tarragon
1 tablespoon chopped
    fresh dill
1 tablespoon
    snipped chives
salt and freshly ground
    black pepper
1 × 500g (1 lb 2 oz)
    packet puff pastry
1kg (2¼ lb) side fresh
    salmon, skinned
1 egg, beaten
6 tablespoons full-fat
    mayonnaise
150ml (¼ pint) double
    cream

PREPARE AHEAD

Can be made up to a day ahead.
Not suitable for freezing.

CONVENTIONAL OVEN

Bake on a hot baking sheet
in an oven preheated to
200°C/Fan 180°C/Gas 6
for 30–40 minutes.

1 Bring a pan of salted water to the boil on the Boiling Plate, add the asparagus and blanch for 3 minutes until just tender. Drain and refresh in cold water. Drain again and put to one side.

2 Spoon the cream cheese into a mixing bowl, add the egg yolk, lemon zest and half the chopped herbs, season with salt and pepper and mix well.

3 Roll the pastry out to 50 × 40cm (20 × 16 in) on a floured work surface. Slice in half lengthways and put one half on a piece of non-stick paper on a baking sheet. Place the side of salmon on top and brush the pastry round it with beaten egg. Spread the salmon with half the cream cheese mixture. Arrange the dry asparagus on top lengthways, covering the whole side of the salmon. Spread the remaining cream cheese mixture over the asparagus spears, carefully pushing between the gaps.

4 Roll the remaining piece of pastry to 30 × 40cm (12 × 16 in) so it is a little bigger than the base piece. Lay on top of the asparagus and seal the edges. Trim to leave a 2cm (¾ in) border all the way round and then crimp the edges. Brush the top of the pastry with beaten egg and decorate with any pastry trimmings to give a lattice effect.

5 Slide the baking sheet on to the floor of the Roasting Oven for 30 minutes, turning around halfway through, until golden and crisp. Rest for 10–15 minutes before serving.

6 To make the sauce, put the remaining herbs in a bowl with the mayonnaise, double cream and lemon juice, season with salt and pepper, and mix to combine. Carve the salmon into slices and serve with the sauce.

Oven-grilled Dover Sole and Other Fish

At last we have found the Aga answer to grilled Dover sole, especially for more than two fish. You can use the same method for other unskinned sole, plaice or salmon cutlets and steaks. Great news, too – you can part-cook them ahead with success every time, then reheat later.

butter, softened
whole Dover soles,
    skinned
salt and freshly ground
    black pepper

1 Melt some butter in either the large or small roasting tin in the Roasting Oven – the size of tin depends on how many soles you are cooking. Use enough butter to give a thin layer over the base of the tin.

2 Preheat an ungreased grill pan on the Boiling Plate until very, very hot. (Take great care to use an oven glove if heating the pan in the oven, as the handle will of course become exceedingly hot.)

3 Spread the soles on the fattest side with soft butter. Take each sole and lightly press the buttered side on to the grill pan so that brown grid marks appear on the sole. This will take 1 or 2 minutes. Dip the fish in the melted butter, season and place in the buttered tin grilled side uppermost. Place the tin on the floor of the Roasting Oven for 8–12 minutes until the fish are done.

4 Serve immediately.

PREPARE AHEAD
Grill the sole on one side, put in the roasting tin with butter as in step 3 and then refrigerate. Do this during the morning to serve in the evening. Reheat on the floor of the Roasting Oven for about 10–13 minutes.

CONVENTIONAL OVEN
Cook under a preheated grill in the usual way.

Seared Fillet of Sea Bass with Tomato and Avocado Salsa

If liked, the salsa may be served hot. Take care only
to bring it to piping hot, do not cook it.

4 × 150g (5 oz) fillets
of sea bass or red
mullet, skin on
olive oil
salt and freshly ground
black pepper
a handful of fresh basil
leaves, shredded
at the last moment

SALSA
4 tablespoons olive oil
2 tablespoons water
1 shallot, quartered
1 large garlic clove,
cut into 8
1 bunch of parsley
stalks
a few basil stalks
1 large avocado,
a fraction under-ripe
1 lime, halved
2 tomatoes, skinned,
deseeded and cut
into thin strips
2 teaspoons capers
(optional)
1 teaspoon caster sugar
salt and freshly ground
black pepper

1 For the salsa, put the oil, water, shallot, garlic,
parsley and basil stalks into a small pan. Cover
and place in the Simmering Oven for 20 minutes
to allow the flavours to infuse. Strain, then cool.

2 Cut the avocado in half and then peel. Remove
the stone, place the cut side of the avocado down
on a board and cut in slices, then toss in the juice
of one lime half.

3 Add the tomato strips, capers (if using), avocado
and sugar to the infused olive oil mixture. Season.

4 Lightly brush the fish fillets with olive oil and
season with salt and pepper.

5 Preheat a ridged grill pan, first on the Simmering
Plate, then the Boiling Plate until piping hot. Lay the
fillets flesh side down on the hot grill pan and cook for
45 seconds, then turn on to the skin side, cover the pan
with a lid, and continue cooking for about 4–5 minutes,
depending on the thickness of the fish. (It is better to
undercook as it can be returned to the pan, but there
is no remedy for overcooked fish.)

6 Place the fillets on four plates, spoon the salsa to
one side of the fish and garnish with shredded leaves
of basil and wedges cut from the remaining half lime.

PREPARE AHEAD
Best made and served
immediately.

CONVENTIONAL OVEN
Cook on the hob in the
usual way.

Smoked Haddock Gratin

An all-in-one dish, perfect for preparing ahead. Buy undyed
smoked haddock – the dye is a fake yellow in colour.

a knob of butter
½ small fennel bulb,
   sliced thinly
400g (14 oz) button
   mushrooms,
   thickly sliced
25g (1 oz) cornflour
750g (1 lb 10 oz) undyed
   smoked haddock,
   skinned, sliced
   into pieces
salt and freshly ground
   black pepper
4 hard-boiled eggs,
   peeled and sliced
100g (4 oz) panko
   breadcrumbs
paprika, for dusting

SAUCE

50g (2 oz) butter
50g (2 oz) plain flour
600ml (1 pint) hot milk
1 teaspoon Dijon
   mustard
125g (4½ oz) Cheddar
   cheese, grated
salt and freshly ground
   black pepper

1 You will need a 2 litre (3½ pint) ovenproof dish.

2 To make the sauce, measure the butter into a pan
and melt on the Boiling Plate. Whisk in the flour
and cook for a minute. Gradually add the hot milk,
whisking until thickened and boiling. Remove from
the heat, whisk in the mustard and 75g (3 oz) of the
cheese and season with salt and pepper.

3 Melt the knob of butter in a frying pan on the
Boiling Plate, add the fennel and fry quickly for 3 minutes.
Add the mushrooms and fry for 2 minutes. Stir in 5
tablespoons of the cheese sauce and then spread this
mixture over the base of the ovenproof dish.

4 Measure the cornflour into a mixing bowl, add the
fish, season with pepper and toss to coat. Scatter the
fish over the mushroom mixture. Arrange the eggs
on top and pour over the remaining cheese sauce.

5 Mix the breadcrumbs with the remaining grated
cheese and sprinkle over the top. Dust with paprika.

6 Bake on the second set of runners in the Roasting
Oven for about 30–35 minutes until golden and
bubbling and the fish is cooked.

7 Serve hot with a green vegetable or a dressed salad.

PREPARE AHEAD
Can be made completely up
to 8 hours ahead. Freezes
well uncooked.

CONVENTIONAL OVEN
Bake in an oven preheated to
200°C/Fan 180°C/Gas 6 for
about 35 minutes until golden.

Salmon, Chilli and Lime Fish Cakes

The fish cakes are oven baked with no additional butter other than a generous greasing of the oven tray. They freeze well before cooking and can be eaten for breakfast, lunch or supper! You can fry the fish cakes in a little oil and butter if preferred.

500g (1 lb 2 oz) potatoes, Desirée or King Edwards, peeled weight
salt and freshly ground black pepper
500g (1 lb 2 oz) fresh skinless salmon fillets
a knob of butter
2 tablespoons full-fat mayonnaise
2 tablespoons chopped fresh coriander
finely grated zest and juice of ½ a large lime
1 red chilli, deseeded and finely diced
75g (3 oz) panko breadcrumbs

1 Cut the potatoes into even sizes and boil in salted water on the Boiling Plate for 5 minutes. Drain, cover and transfer to the Simmering Oven until tender, about 40 minutes. Drain any excess water created, and mash with the buttery juices from the fish when it is cooked.

2 Season the fish with salt and pepper. Cut the fillets in half if they are large. Wrap the fish in a foil parcel with a good 30g (1¼ oz) butter. Bake on the grid shelf on the floor of the Roasting Oven for 10–12 minutes or until the fish is opaque and flakes in the centre when tested with a fork.

3 Flake the fish into a bowl with the mashed potatoes, discarding any bones. Add the rest of the ingredients, apart from the breadcrumbs. Taste and season well with salt and pepper. Allow the mixture to cool, then put into the fridge until firm enough to shape.

4 Divide the mixture into twelve even-sized fish cakes and roll in breadcrumbs. Cover and chill if time allows.

5 Preheat a baking sheet covered with a piece of baking parchment on the floor of the Roasting Oven. Generously butter the hot paper using kitchen paper. Bake the fish cakes in the Roasting Oven for 4 minutes, turn over and bake for a further 4 minutes until golden brown and piping hot. (If you don't preheat the baking sheet the fish cakes are apt to spread.) Alternatively, fry on the Boiling Plate in some butter.

PREPARE AHEAD

Prepare the fish cakes up to 2 days ahead to the end of step 4. They also freeze well for up to 2 months.

CONVENTIONAL OVEN

Bake the parcel of fish in an oven preheated to 200°C/ Fan 180°C/Gas 6 for 12–15 minutes until the fish is opaque and flakes easily. Make and shape the fish cakes as above. Preheat a heavy baking sheet in the oven. Lightly grease with butter and put the fish cakes in a single layer, brush with melted butter, then cook at 220°C/Fan 200°C/Gas 7 for 20 minutes until crisp, golden and hot through.

VARIATIONS

Using the ingredients below, follow the recipe opposite.

SALMON AND FRESH HERB FISH CAKES

550g (1¼ lb) potatoes, Desirée or King Edwards, peeled weight
salt and freshly ground black pepper
450g (1 lb) fresh skinless salmon fillets
about 50g (2 oz) butter
2 good tablespoons light mayonnaise
3 heaped tablespoons chopped fresh parsley
1 heaped tablespoon chopped fresh dill
2 drops Tabasco sauce
75g (3 oz) panko breadcrumbs

SMOKED HADDOCK NEW YORK FISH CAKES

500g (1 lb 2 oz) potatoes, Desirée or King Edwards, peeled weight
salt and freshly ground black pepper
500g (1 lb 2 oz) undyed smoked haddock fillet
2 tablespoons full-fat mayonnaise
100g (4 oz) small gherkins, finely chopped
1 tablespoon capers, chopped
1 teaspoon Dijon mustard
2 tablespoons chopped fresh parsley
75g (3 oz) panko breadcrumbs

ROASTING CHARTS

Roasts are perfect in the Aga: crisp outside and beautifully moist on the inside.

CHICKEN

Lightly smear the chicken with soft butter or sunflower oil. Season. Put an onion, a whole lemon cut in halves or herbs in the cavity. Stuff the breast end, if liked. Stand on a grill rack in a roasting tin. Cover breast with foil but remove it to brown.

Slide the tin on to the lowest set of runners in the Roasting Oven.

small (900g/2 lb) about 45 minutes
medium (1.3kg/3 lb) about 1 hour
large (1.8kg/4 lb) about 1½ hours

To see if it is cooked, pierce the thickest part of the thigh with a small sharp knife and if the juices run clear then the chicken is done; if still pink cook for a little longer.

TURKEY

To prepare the turkey for the oven, stuff the breast end with any meat stuffing and the body cavity with non-meat stuffing. Lightly butter the bird. Lift into the large roasting tin – putting on a grill rack if liked. Leave untrussed. Loosely cover with foil.

There are two methods of cooking turkey in the Aga. The slow overnight method not only gives a very moist bird but leaves the Roasting Oven free to cook all the other trimmings that go with the turkey. Rest the bird for 15 minutes covered with foil before serving. If your Aga Simmering Oven is slow it is advisable to lightly brown the turkey in the Roasting Oven first.

SLOW ROASTING

Place on the grid shelf on the floor of the Simmering Oven:

3.5–4.5kg (8–10 lb) about 8–10 hours
5–7.25kg (11–16 lb) about 9–12 hours
7.5–10kg (17–22 lb) about 10–14 hours
over 10kg (22 lb) start in the Roasting Oven until lightly browned (about 30 minutes), cover loosely with foil and transfer to the Simmering Oven for 11–16 hours

Take the turkey out of the oven, pierce the thickest part of the thigh with a small sharp knife – if the juices run clear then the turkey is done; if they are still tinged with pink then cook for a little longer. If in doubt use a meat thermometer to check.

Drain off the liquid from the tin, skim off the fat and keep the stock for gravy. Remove the foil. Transfer the bird to the Roasting Oven to brown the skin.

FAST ROASTING

Cover with foil and cook in the large roasting tin on the lowest set of runners in the Roasting Oven.

3.5–4.5kg (8–10 lb) about 1¾–2 hours
5–7.25kg (11–16 lb) about 2½ hours
7.5–10kg (17–22 lb) about 3 hours

Baste the bird from time to time. Remove the foil 30 minutes before the end of cooking to crisp the skin. Test that the bird is done as above.

DUCK OR GOOSE

It is better to buy two smaller ducks at 4.5–5kg (10–11 lb) rather than one large (also two smaller geese rather than one large). Each duck serves 6–8.

Prick the skin and place upside down on the grill rack in the roasting tin. Place on the lowest set of runners in the Roasting Oven and cook until brown on the underside (goose about 30 minutes, duck about 20 minutes). Reverse to sit the right way up and brown the breast. The time will vary but cook for less than the underside. Transfer to the Simmering Oven until tender (goose about 2 hours, duck about 1 hour). Return to the Roasting Oven to crisp the skin.

PHEASANT

Put a brace of young pheasants in a roasting tin, rub with butter, season and lay a rasher of streaky bacon over each breast.

Hang the tin on the middle set of runners in the Roasting Oven and cook, basting once, for 45–50 minutes until golden. Take the birds out of the oven, pierce a thigh with a fine skewer – if the juices run clear, they are done.

Serve with game chips, bread sauce or fried breadcrumbs. To make these, fry fresh white breadcrumbs in butter and oil until golden, seasoning well. Also serve gravy made from the stock plus the juices and a fruit jelly, such as redcurrant or apple. Garnish with watercress.

PARTRIDGE

Cook as for pheasant but reduce time to 30–35 minutes as the birds are smaller.

GROUSE

A great luxury these days. Only roast young birds – casserole older ones. Roast as for pheasant but reduce cooking time to 30 minutes or less for a small bird. Serve each bird on a disc of fried bread spread with sautéed grouse liver. Don't leave the bird to stand on the bread for too long as the juices from the bird drain out and make it soggy.

WOODCOCK, SNIPE OR QUAIL

Roast as for pheasant but reduce cooking time to 15 minutes.

ROASTING RED MEAT

There are two methods of roasting — normal and slow roasting. Coarser cuts are better cooked slowly and better cuts are best cooked normally.

A long thin joint such as a boned and rolled loin of pork or lamb will take less time than a solid leg of pork or lamb pound for pound.

Season the meat, place in the small or large roasting tin and on a grill rack if you like. Hang the tin on the lowest set of runners in the Roasting Oven. Before carving, leave the meat to rest for 15 minutes covered in foil.

NORMAL FAST ROASTING METHOD

BEEF

These times give a pink, medium-rare centre. If you like it well done, add 5 minutes per 450g (1 lb).

on the bone 12 minutes per 450g (1 lb)
off the bone 15 minutes per 450g (1 lb)
fillet 10 minutes per 450g (1 lb)

We have found a 900g (2 lb) thick end of fillet takes 25 minutes in the Roasting Oven and 35 minutes for a 1.8kg (4 lb) thick end of fillet for a pink middle. If you like it well done increase the time a little.

PORK

Pork crackling is wonderful when it is just right and very crisp. First see that the skin is freshly scored, then brush with oil or rub over with a butter paper. Sprinkle with salt at the end of the cooking time, or if you prefer at the beginning, roast at the top of the Roasting Oven until the skin bubbles. If it is an awkward shape with some of the crackling under the joint, remove all the skin with a sharp knife before roasting and roast the crackling separately. 25 minutes per 450g (1 lb).

MUTTON

Mutton is difficult to buy but it is worth searching for. We buy ours from a country butcher; it is inexpensive and full of flavour. We stew the smaller cuts of mutton (they take double the time for lamb) but slow roast larger joints. Trim excess fat before cooking. To roast a large shoulder or leg, cook in the roasting tin overnight in the Simmering Oven loosely covered in foil — it will be done by morning. We take it out and drain off all the juices and fat from the tin. Once the fat has set we then use the juices for gravy and reheat the joint and brown it in the Roasting Oven for 30 minutes before lunch. We serve it with caper, mint or onion sauce.

VEAL

Cook as for beef but increase time to 20 minutes per 450g (1 lb).

LAMB

When roasting lamb, sprinkle the top surface with rosemary or pierce little holes with a sharp knife and insert slivers of garlic and rosemary.

pink 15 minutes per 450g (1 lb)
well done 20 minutes per 450g (1 lb)

SLOW ROASTING METHOD

Calculate the cooking time for specific meats by using the information above. Take 30 minutes off the total cooking time for fast roasting, and then double the remaining to work out how long it needs to be in the Simmering Oven.

Cook in the Roasting Oven for about 30 minutes, or until beginning to brown, then transfer to the Simmering Oven. In the case of best cuts of beef, lamb, veal and pork, bring back to the Roasting Oven to crisp before serving. For less tender beef roasts such as silverside or brisket, transfer to the Simmering Oven for 1 hour per 450g (1 lb).

BOILED BACON AND GAMMON JOINTS

I find that when the joints are cooked very slowly, they taste delicious, are moist and lose very little weight due to shrinkage.

Soak joints in cold water for 6 to 12 hours according to size.

Put a small upturned enamel plate in the bottom of a pan so that the joint won't come into contact with the bottom of the pan. Add the joint and cover with fresh cold water, cover, bring slowly to the boil then simmer for 20–30 minutes depending on the size of the joint.

Transfer to the floor of the Simmering Oven for the following length of time (use the floor grid in an **Aga Total Control** or **City60**):

900g–1.3kg (2–3 lb)	about 1½ hours
1.8–2.25kg (4–5 lb)	about 2 hours
2.7–3kg (6–7 lb)	about 2½ hours
3.5–4kg (8–9 lb)	about 3½–4 hours
4.5–5kg (10–11 lb)	about 4½ hours
5.4–6kg (12–13 lb)	about 5 hours
6.3–6.75kg (14–15 lb)	about 5½ hours
7.25kg (16 lb and over)	about 6 hours

Remove from the oven and take out of the water.

To test for doneness, spear with a skewer though to the centre; it should go through easily and juices run clear. Or use a meat thermometer – if the temperature is not reached, i.e. 75°C, return to the water, bring to the boil and return to the Simmering Oven until done.

Cool a little and cut off any string. Peel off the skin and score the fatty surface. Mix dry mustard powder and demerara sugar together and press on to the fatty skin. Cover all the lean meat with foil and stand in a roasting tin.

Brown fairly near the top of the Roasting Oven for about 10–20 minutes, according to size. Do keep an eye on the joint, and turn to get an even colour.

NOTE
MEAT THERMOMETERS

With an Aga, a meat thermometer is a great asset, and they are not expensive to buy from good kitchen stores. It is difficult to give exact cooking instructions when cooking meat, because a long thin piece of meat will cook considerably quicker than a thick dense rolled joint of the same weight. I recommend the use of a meat thermometer to check the internal temperature of the meat so you can gauge the degree of doneness. Put into the thickest part of the meat, not touching the bone, and the thermometer will register the internal heat.

Chicken Curry

Tomato based rather than creamy, this curry has spices
and flavours from India and works equally well
with beef – use 900g (2 lb) cubed chuck steak.

2 tablespoons olive oil
1kg (2¼ lb) chicken
  thighs, boneless, skin
  removed and sliced
  into strips
6 banana shallots, sliced
2 red peppers, deseeded
  and finely diced
1 red chilli, deseeded
  and chopped
3cm (1¼ in) piece fresh
  root ginger, peeled
  and grated
4 garlic cloves, crushed
1 teaspoon ground
  cloves
1 tablespoon ground
  turmeric
1 tablespoon ground
  coriander
1 tablespoon ground
  cumin
2 × 400g (14 oz) tins
  of chopped tomatoes
1 tablespoon tomato
  purée
2 tablespoons mango
  chutney
salt and freshly ground
  black pepper
3 tablespoons natural
  yoghurt, to taste

1 Heat half the oil in a large frying pan on the
Boiling Plate and fry the chicken until brown all
over (you may need to do this in batches). Set aside.

2 Heat the remaining oil in the pan and add
the shallots, peppers and chilli and fry for about
3–4 minutes. Add the ginger and garlic and fry for
another minute. Stir in the spices and fry for another
minute. Finally stir in the tinned tomatoes, purée
and chutney and season with salt and pepper.
Return the chicken to the pan.

3 Bring to the boil, cover and transfer to the
Simmering Oven for about 1–1½ hours, or
until tender and thick.

4 Stir in the yoghurt and serve with rice and
naan bread.

PREPARE AHEAD
Can be made to the end of
step 3 up to 2 days ahead.
It also freezes well for up
to 3 months.

CONVENTIONAL OVEN
Cook on the hob in the usual
way, then transfer to an oven
preheated to 160°C/Fan
140°C/Gas 3 for about an hour.

Mary's Coq au Vin

Still one of our favourite recipes – a modern version of the classic French dish. We have used thighs but you could use 6 chicken breasts, if preferred, and cook for 10 minutes less. Serve with creamy mashed potatoes and green vegetables.

1 bottle of red wine
2 tablespoons olive oil
10–12 chicken thighs,
   skin on, bone in
450g (1 lb) medium
   shallots or pickling
   onions, peeled
   and halved
3 large sticks of celery,
   sliced fairly thinly
100g (4 oz) pancetta,
   chopped
3 garlic cloves, crushed
25g (1 oz) plain flour
150ml (¼ pint) chicken
   stock
1–2 tablespoons
   redcurrant jelly
salt and freshly ground
   black pepper
a knob of butter
100g (4 oz) button
   mushrooms, left
   whole

1 Pour the wine into a wide-based pan and bring to the boil on the Boiling Plate. Leave to reduce by half and then set aside.

2 Heat the oil in a large pan on the Boiling Plate and fry the chicken until golden all over (you may need to do this in batches). Lift out with a slotted spoon and set aside.

3 Add the shallots, celery, pancetta and garlic to the pan and fry for a few minutes until starting to colour.

4 Measure the flour into a small bowl, mix with 2 tablespoons of cold water and stir until smooth. Tip into a large mixing bowl and pour in the reduced wine and stock and mix together well. Pour into the frying pan, stir to thicken and bring to the boil. Add the redcurrant jelly and return the chicken to the pan. Bring back to the boil, season, cover and transfer to the Simmering Oven for about 45 minutes or until the chicken is cooked through.

5 When ready to serve, melt the butter in a pan on the Boiling Plate and fry the mushrooms until golden. Stir into the chicken and serve.

PREPARE AHEAD
This dish can be made completely up to 2 days ahead. It also freezes well for up to 3 months. Add the mushrooms when reheating.

CONVENTIONAL OVEN
Bring to the boil on the hob and then transfer to an oven preheated to 160°C/Fan 140°C/Gas 3 for about 45 minutes until the chicken is cooked through.

Chicken Breasts with Leek, Potatoes and Thyme

This is a prepare-ahead dish, perfect for all the family.

350g (12 oz) baby
  new potatoes
salt and freshly ground
  black pepper
4 thin leeks, cut into
  2cm (¾ in) slices
6 small chicken breasts,
  skinless and boneless
1 tablespoon olive oil
1 tablespoon runny
  honey
50g (2 oz) butter
1 onion, thinly sliced
1 garlic clove, crushed
50g (2 oz) flour
450ml (16 fl oz)
  apple juice
200ml (⅓ pint) full-fat
  crème fraiche
1 tablespoon chopped
  fresh thyme leaves
2 tablespoons chopped
  fresh parsley

PREPARE AHEAD

Can be made up to a day
ahead. Freezes well without
the potato for up to 2 months.

CONVENTIONAL OVEN

Bake in an oven preheated
to 200°C/Fan 180°C/Gas 6
for up to 25 minutes. Remove
the foil and cook for a further
10 minutes.

1 You will need a 2.3 litre (4 pint) ovenproof
dish, buttered.

2 Put the potatoes into a pan, cover with cold water,
add salt and bring to the boil on the Boiling Plate.
Boil for 12 minutes, then add the leeks to the water
and boil for a further 3 minutes or until the potatoes
are just tender. Drain in a colander.

3 Season the chicken with salt and pepper. Heat the
oil in a large frying pan on the Boiling Plate. Add
the chicken and drizzle with honey. Quickly brown
the chicken for a few minutes on each side until
golden. Remove with a slotted spoon and set aside.

4 Add the butter to the unwashed frying pan. Add
the onion and garlic and fry on the Boiling Plate for a
minute. Cover with a lid and transfer to the Simmering
Oven for 10 minutes. Remove the lid, return to the
Boiling Plate and fry for a minute. Sprinkle in the flour,
stir in the apple juice and mix until smooth. Add the
crème fraîche and thyme and season with salt and
pepper. Stir until thickened and bring to the boil.

5 Remove from the heat, add the leeks and potatoes
and stir to mix. Tip into the dish and sit the chicken
on top. Cover with foil and seal the edges.

6 Bake on the grid shelf on the floor of the
Roasting Oven for 20 minutes. Remove the foil
and cook for a further 8–10 minutes or until
the chicken is cooked through.

7 Sprinkle with the parsley and serve with
a green vegetable.

Chicken with Madeira and Tarragon Sauce

This recipe also works well with guinea fowl or young pheasants. Tarragon is particularly good here. Make sure you find French rather than Russian tarragon, as the latter is flavourless.

40g (1½ oz) butter
1 tablespoon
   sunflower oil
8 chicken thighs,
   skinned
225g (8 oz) shallots,
   finely chopped
25g (1 oz) plain flour
300ml (½ pint)
   chicken stock
100ml (4 fl oz) Madeira
salt and freshly ground
   black pepper
1 × 200ml (7 fl oz)
   carton of full-fat
   crème fraîche
1 scant tablespoon
   chopped fresh
   tarragon

1 Put the butter and oil in a large frying pan on the Boiling Plate, and brown the chicken until golden. Lift out of the pan with a slotted spoon and set aside.

2 Add the shallots to the frying pan and brown quickly. Lift out and put with the chicken. Transfer the pan to the Simmering Plate.

3 Whisk the flour into the fat and juices remaining in the pan. Slowly add the stock and then the Madeira. Season well, and return the chicken joints and shallots to the pan. Bring to the boil on the Boiling Plate, cover and transfer to the Simmering Oven until tender, about 35 minutes.

4 Arrange the chicken on a serving dish and keep warm. Skim off any fat from the sauce, add the crème fraîche and bring back to the boil on the Boiling Plate. Check the seasoning and add most of the tarragon. Pour the sauce over the chicken and sprinkle with a little more tarragon to serve.

PREPARE AHEAD
The completed dish can be made up to a day ahead and reheated. It also freezes well for up to 1 month.

CONVENTIONAL OVEN
Cook in an oven preheated to 180°C/Fan 160°C/Gas 4 for about 20–25 minutes until cooked through.

Chicken Cassoulet

This is a modern, lighter version of a traditional cassoulet recipe. It has a hint of chilli and pancetta.

1 tablespoon chopped
   fresh thyme leaves
6 teaspoons sun-dried
   tomato paste
4 chicken breasts,
   boneless and skinned
salt and freshly ground
   black pepper
3 tablespoons olive oil
1 onion, finely chopped
2 garlic cloves, crushed
½–1 red chilli, deseeded
   and sliced
75g (3 oz) pancetta,
   diced
150ml (¼ pint)
   white wine
1 × 400g (14 oz) tin
   of chopped tomatoes
1 × 400g (14 oz) tin of
   butter beans, drained
   and rinsed
1 tablespoon chopped
   fresh parsley

1 Mix half the thyme leaves with 4 teaspoons of the sun-dried tomato paste, and spread a teaspoonful on each chicken breast. Season the chicken well.

2 Heat 2 tablespoons of the olive oil in a large frying pan on the Boiling Plate. Add the chicken and pan fry for a few minutes on each side until golden brown. Remove and set aside.

3 Add the remaining oil to the frying pan and stir in the onion, garlic and chilli. Fry for a few minutes until starting to turn golden. Cover and transfer to the Simmering Oven for about 10 minutes, until the onion is soft.

4 Return to the Boiling Plate, add the pancetta and fry until crisp. Mix the wine, tomatoes and remaining tomato paste together and pour into the pan. Add the browned chicken and bring to the boil. Cover and transfer to the Simmering Oven for 15 minutes. Stir in the beans and return to the Simmering Oven for a further 15 minutes, until the chicken is tender.

5 Remove from the oven, add the parsley and remaining thyme, and check the seasoning. Serve immediately.

PREPARE AHEAD
The dish can be made up to 2 days ahead. It also freezes well for up to 2 months.

CONVENTIONAL OVEN
Cook on the hob in the usual way.

Hot American Chicken Salad

A very easy recipe – take great care not to cook for too long otherwise the sauce will curdle. This recipe makes the last cuts from a roast chicken into something special. Cook as required as the cooking time is short. Garnish with fresh tarragon or parsley.

350g (12 oz) cooked chicken, diced
4 sticks of celery, finely sliced
4 spring onions, finely sliced
300ml (½ pint) full-fat mayonnaise
2 teaspoons lemon juice
salt and freshly ground black pepper

TOPPING
100g (4 oz) well-flavoured Cheddar cheese, grated
1 packet potato crisps, crumbled
paprika

1 Measure all the salad ingredients into a bowl, together with 75g (3 oz) of the cheese. Season and blend together. Turn into a shallow ovenproof dish. Top with the remaining cheese, crisps and a dusting of paprika.

2 Slide on to the second set of runners in the Roasting Oven, cook for about 10–15 minutes until hot. Don't cook longer otherwise the sauce will separate. Serve straight away.

PREPARE AHEAD
Step 1 can be done up to a day ahead but the dish must be cooked to serve.

CONVENTIONAL OVEN
Cook in an oven preheated to 200°C/Fan 180°C/Gas 6 for about 10–15 minutes until hot.

Curried Chicken Salad

Similar to Coronation chicken, this is perfect for large numbers or a summer buffet. It is also a lovely way to use up leftover roast chicken – simply substitute the raw chicken with 350g (12 oz) cooked chicken strips and omit steps 1 and 2.

750g (1 lb 10 oz)
  chicken breasts,
  on the bone, skinless
1 stock cube

SAUCE

8 tablespoons light
  mayonnaise
8 tablespoons natural
  yoghurt
3 tablespoons medium
  curry powder
3 tablespoons mango
  chutney
a squeeze of lemon juice
½ teaspoon grated
  fresh ginger
salt and freshly ground
  black pepper

PREPARE AHEAD

Can be made up to a day ahead. The sauce can be made up to 3 days ahead.

CONVENTIONAL OVEN

Poach the chicken on the hob in the usual way.

1 Put the chicken in a saucepan, cover with water and crumble in the stock cube. Bring to the boil on the Boiling Plate, cover and transfer to the Simmering Oven for about 20 minutes to poach the chicken until cooked through.

2 Remove the chicken from the liquid and set aside to cool. Slice into long thin strips.

3 To make the sauce, measure the ingredients into a bowl, season with salt and pepper and stir to combine. Add the chicken and toss together.

4 Serve with dressed lettuce leaves and crusty bread.

VARIATION

CHICKEN CAESAR SALAD

8 tablespoons light mayonnaise
8 tablespoons natural yoghurt
1 tablespoon Dijon mustard
1 garlic clove, crushed
1 teaspoon Worcestershire sauce
50g (2 oz) Parmesan cheese, grated
6 spring onions, sliced

1 Mix all the ingredients together and add to the poached chicken.

Pheasant with Orange and Chestnuts

The timing of this recipe is for roasting young birds, but you can use old birds or ones you have got from a shoot – they may well take 4–5 hours to get really tender.

2 tablespoons
  sunflower oil
25g (1 oz) butter
a brace of young
  roasting pheasants
175g (6 oz) dried
  chestnuts, soaked
  overnight in cold
  water then strained
50g (2 oz) flour
300ml (½ pint) red wine
600ml (1 pint) good
  game stock
2 onions, quartered
1 orange, thinly peeled
  rind and juice
2 teaspoons redcurrant
  jelly
salt and freshly ground
  black pepper

1 Heat 1 tablespoon of the oil in a large pan with the butter and fry the pheasants on the Boiling Plate until browned all over. Lift out with a slotted spoon and set aside.

2 Add the remaining oil to the pan with the chestnuts and fry quickly to brown. Lift out with a slotted spoon and add to the pheasant.

3 Whisk in the flour to the remaining fat in the pan and cook gently for a minute. Stir in the wine and stock and bring to the boil, stirring until thickened. Add the onions to the pan with the orange rind, juice, redcurrant jelly and seasoning, and blend together.

4 Return the pheasants and chestnuts to the pan, cover with a lid and bring back to the boil. Simmer for about 10 minutes.

5 Transfer the pan to the floor of the Simmering Oven for about 2 hours. The timing will depend largely on the age of the birds. Taste to check seasoning and remove the rind before serving.

PREPARE AHEAD
This dish can be made completely ahead and also freezes well.

CONVENTIONAL OVEN
Start cooking on the hob in the usual way. Transfer the casserole to an oven preheated to 160°C/Fan 140°C/Gas 3 for about 3–4 hours.

Duck Breasts with Wild Mushroom Sauce

Duck breasts are such a perfect dish for entertaining – smart but easy.

15g (½ oz) dried
   wild mushrooms
6 duck breasts,
   skin removed
salt and freshly ground
   black pepper
a knob of butter
50ml (2 fl oz) brandy
200ml (⅓ pint)
   double cream
2 teaspoons mango
   chutney
2 teaspoons chopped
   fresh thyme
a few drops
   Worcestershire sauce

1 Put the dried mushrooms and 300ml (½ pint) of water into a pan. Bring to the boil, cover and boil for 2 minutes on the Boiling Plate. Set aside for about 20 minutes to infuse.

2 Meanwhile, heat a frying pan on the Boiling Plate. Season the duck, add butter to the pan and brown the breasts on both sides for about a minute. Transfer to a small roasting tin but keep the frying pan to one side.

3 Roast the duck on the grid shelf on the floor of the Roasting Oven for about 6 minutes.

4 Drain the dried mushroom liquid into a jug and pour into the frying pan. Chop the mushrooms and add to the frying pan. Boil on the Boiling Plate to reduce by half.

5 Add the brandy to the pan and reduce again for 2 minutes. Add the cream, chutney, thyme and Worcestershire sauce, and bring back to the boil, stirring until reduced and thickened. Add the duck juices and check the seasoning.

6 Carve the duck breasts thinly and serve with the sauce.

PREPARE AHEAD
The sauce can be made up to 1 day ahead, then reheated and the juices added.

CONVENTIONAL OVEN
Cook the duck breasts on the hob for 3 minutes on each side.

Highland Venison

Venison for stewing is very lean, reasonable in price and so good. We find it best if marinated in the fridge for at least 48 hours but make sure you don't use a metal bowl as the acid in the wine can taint the marinade.

900g (2 lb) stewing
venison, cut into
2.5cm (1 in) cubes
300ml (½ pint) red wine
2 bay leaves
25g (1 oz) butter
1 tablespoon
sunflower oil
1 large onion, chopped
25g (1 oz) flour
300ml (½ pint) stock
100g (4 oz) German
smoked sausage,
sliced
1 tablespoon redcurrant
jelly
salt and freshly ground
black pepper
175g (6 oz) button
mushrooms, sliced

1 Put the venison in a glass or china bowl with the red wine and bay leaves, cover and leave to marinate in the fridge for about 48 hours.

2 Strain the red wine from the venison and keep. Discard the bay leaves.

3 Measure the butter and oil into a large pan, cook the onion gently on the Simmering Plate for about 10 minutes, then stir in the flour and cook for a minute. Gradually blend in the stock and reserved red wine. Bring to the boil, stirring until thickened. Stir in the venison with the smoked sausage, redcurrant jelly and seasoning. Bring back to the boil and cover with a lid. Simmer for 5 minutes.

4 Cook on the floor of the Simmering Oven for about 4 hours, or until the venison is tender, adding the mushrooms for the last 30 minutes or so of cooking.

5 Serve with creamy mashed potato and a green vegetable.

PREPARE AHEAD
The casserole can be made completely up to 2 days ahead. It can also be frozen for up to 2 months.

CONVENTIONAL OVEN
Cook on the hob in the usual way and then transfer to an oven preheated to 160°C/Fan 140°C/Gas 3 for about 4 hours or until tender.

Spiced Treacle Gammon

Choose smoked or unsmoked gammon, on or off the bone, whichever appeals to you most. Once gammon is cooked, it is called ham – confusing! Cooking the gammon overnight means that the Aga is free during the day to do other cooking. In Mary's Aga the gammon is tender after 13 hours so she starts cooking it at about 8.30 pm after she's taken whatever is in the Simmering Oven out for supper. The gammon is cooked by about 9.30 the next morning, and just needs skinning and browning. It is best to use a meat thermometer to check when it is done.

a whole gammon,
   about 7.25kg (16 lb)
black treacle
25g (1 oz) black
   peppercorns, crushed
English mustard
   powder
demerara sugar

PREPARE AHEAD
Cool quickly after cooking, wrap loosely in foil and keep for up to 1 week in the fridge. Not suitable for freezing.

CONVENTIONAL OVEN
Cook in an oven preheated to 160°C/Fan 140°C/Gas 3 for 20 minutes per 450g (1 lb). A meat thermometer should register 75°C/170°F. To glaze, increase the temperature of the oven to 230°C/Fan 210°C/Gas 8 for 15–20 minutes until brown.

1 Soak the gammon in plenty of cold water for 24 hours.

2 Take a large piece of foil – twice the size of the large roasting tin – and line the tin with it, letting the foil overlap. Lift the gammon on top and spread with black treacle. Sprinkle with the crushed peppercorns and loosely fold the foil over the top. Slide the roasting tin on to the floor of the Simmering Oven (use the floor grid in an Aga Total Control or City60). Cook overnight, for about 14 hours (maybe longer in a slow, older Aga). Check first thing in the morning.

3 Open the foil, pierce the gammon with a skewer in the thickest part and if the skewer goes in easily and the juices that flow out are clear, it is done. If the centre feels firm and the juices are pink, cook for longer. Or you can test the meat with a meat thermometer – it should register 75°C/170°F.

4 Remove the foil, throw away the salty juices and peel off the skin when cool enough to handle. Score the fat diagonally with a sharp knife and stand the gammon on a new piece of foil in the roasting tin. Sprinkle with mustard powder and demerara sugar. Slide on to the lowest set of runners in the Roasting Oven. Roast until brown, about 20 minutes, and serve hot, or allow to cool.

Roast Pork Belly

Perfect slow cooking – leave to cook in the Aga while you go for a walk or to the pub! If you find carving tricky, run the knife under the crackling and snip with scissors to serve. Carve the meat as normal.

1.5kg (3 lb 5 oz) pork
   belly, skin on
   and scored
salt
1 large onion, cut
   into wedges
700ml (1¼ pint) hot
   chicken stock
a knob of butter
2 tablespoons flour
freshly ground
   black pepper
a dash of sugar
a dash of gravy
   browning

PREPARE AHEAD

Best cooked to serve.

CONVENTIONAL OVEN

Roast in an oven preheated to 220°C/Fan 200°C/Gas 7 for about 45 minutes, then reduce the temperature to 150°C/Fan 130°C/Gas 2 for about 3–4 hours. Increase to 220°C/Fan 200°C/Gas 7 for 20–30 minutes, or until the skin is really crispy.

1 Rub the skin of the pork with lots of salt. Put the onion pieces in the middle of a small roasting tin in a pile. Sit the pork on top (so the onion acts like a trivet). Slide on to the highest set of runners in the Roasting Oven for about 45 minutes or until the skin is golden all over and starting to crisp around the edges.

2 Add 300ml (½ pint) of the chicken stock to the base of the tin and transfer to the Simmering Oven for about 3–4 hours, or until completely tender and falling apart.

3 Slide back on to the top set of runners in the Roasting Oven for about 20–30 minutes, or until the skin is really crispy.

4 Transfer the meat to a carving board, cover and rest.

5 Strain any juices from the pan through a sieve into a jug. Add the remaining chicken stock until you have 450ml (16 fl oz) of liquid.

6 Put a knob of butter into a saucepan and melt on the Boiling Plate. Add the flour and whisk to combine. Gradually pour in the stock and juices, whisking until thickened. Check the seasoning and add a dash of sugar to taste and a little gravy browning to cheer up the colour.

7 Carve the pork and serve with the gravy and buttered, pan-fried apples, if liked.

Toad in the Hole

The secret behind a really good Toad in the Hole is to ensure that the Aga is right up to temperature. This way the batter will rise beautifully.

2 tablespoons
  sunflower oil
12 good-quality
  pork sausages

BATTER
75g (3 oz) plain flour
2 eggs
150ml (¼ pint) milk
salt and freshly ground
  black pepper

1 Lightly grease the small roasting tin with oil around the base and sides.

2 To make the batter, measure the flour into a bowl. Make a well in the centre and add the eggs. Whisk with a hand whisk and gradually add the milk until combined to give a smooth batter. Season with salt and pepper.

3 Sit the sausages in the roasting tin and roast on the second set of runners in the Roasting Oven for about 25 minutes, until golden on one side. Drain half the fat into a bowl, turn the sausages over and pour the batter around the sausages. Return to the same position in the oven for about 30 minutes, or until the batter is well risen, crisp and golden brown.

PREPARE AHEAD
The batter can be made up to 12 hours ahead.

CONVENTIONAL OVEN
Cook as above in an oven preheated to 200°C/Fan 180°C/Gas 6.

Pork Steaks with a Quick Mushroom and Mustard Sauce

Steaks and chops are easy to cook in the Aga but they can also be grilled using the Aga grill pan on the Boiling Plate.

6 pork loin steaks
salt and freshly ground
    black pepper
1 tablespoon runny
    honey
2 tablespoons oil
a knob of butter
1 shallot, sliced
20g (7 oz) button
    mushrooms, sliced
200ml (⅓ pint)
    apple juice
200ml (⅓ pint)
    double cream
1–2 tablespoons
    grainy mustard

1 Season the pork steaks and drizzle with honey on both sides.

2 Heat the oil in a large frying pan on the Boiling Plate. Fry the steaks for 1–2 minutes, or until golden on each side. Transfer to a roasting tin and slide on to the grid shelf on the floor of the Roasting Oven and cook for 4–5 minutes, or until cooked. Transfer to a plate to rest.

3 Add the butter and shallot to the pan and fry for 3 minutes on the Boiling Plate. Add the mushrooms and continue to fry for 2 minutes. Pour in the apple juice and boil to reduce by half. Stir in the cream and boil until of a coating consistency. Finally stir in the mustard and check the seasoning.

4 Serve the steaks with the sauce and some buttery mash and greens.

PREPARE AHEAD
The sauce can be made up to a day ahead. Add the pork juice once the pork is cooked. Do not freeze.

CONVENTIONAL OVEN
Cook on the hob in the usual way.

Sticky Spare Ribs

These are great in the Aga as the Simmering Oven makes them tender and the Roasting Oven gives a sticky glaze. These are Lucy's husband's favourite so have been very well tested!

12 pork ribs
2cm (¾ in) piece root ginger, peeled and finely grated
100ml (3½ fl oz) soy sauce
50ml (2 fl oz) hoisin sauce
2 tablespoons runny honey
2 tablespoons sunflower oil

1 Lay the ribs in a shallow dish. Measure the remaining ingredients into a bowl and mix together. Spread over the ribs, cover and marinate in the fridge for a minimum of 30 minutes.

2 To roast, arrange the ribs and their marinade in a large roasting tin. Slide on to the floor of the Roasting Oven and cook for about 30–35 minutes or until brown.

3 Pour 150ml (¼ pint) water into the base of the tin (being careful not to pour it over the ribs). Cover the whole dish with foil and transfer to the Simmering Oven for about an hour.

4 Remove the foil, return to the floor of the Roasting Oven for about 5–10 minutes or until the ribs are sticky with the glaze.

5 Serve hot with corn on the cob and coleslaw.

PREPARE AHEAD
Can be marinated up to 12 hours ahead. The ribs freeze well marinated but uncooked.

CONVENTIONAL OVEN
Roast in an oven preheated to 200°C/Fan 180°C/Gas 6 for 30 minutes. Cover with foil, reduce the temperature to 160°C/Fan 140°C/Gas 3 for about an hour. Pour the pan juices into a saucepan, boil on the hob to reduce and pour over the cooked ribs to serve.

Pork Noodle Stir-fry

Stir-fries cook so well on the Aga. The Boiling Plate is an intense heat, which is perfect if you use the correct pan – a wide-based, deep pan or wok is ideal. It helps to chill the fillet before slicing into strips.

150g (5 oz) medium egg noodles

300g (10 oz) pork fillet, sliced into thin strips

salt and freshly ground black pepper

3 tablespoons runny honey

3 tablespoons sesame oil

1 teaspoon cornflour

4 tablespoons soy sauce

1 tablespoon rice wine vinegar

2 tablespoons olive oil

1 tablespoon grated fresh ginger

200g (7 oz) button mushrooms, sliced

6 spring onions, sliced

1 red pepper, deseeded and sliced

200g (7 oz) mangetout, sliced

35g (1¼ oz) cashew nuts, toasted and roughly chopped

1 Cook the noodles on the Boiling Plate according to the packet instructions. Drain and refresh in cold water to stop them cooking.

2 Season the pork and drizzle over 2 tablespoons of the runny honey.

3 Heat 2 tablespoons of the sesame oil in a deep, wide-based pan on the Boiling Plate and fry the pork until golden brown all over. Remove with a slotted spoon and keep to one side.

4 Measure the cornflour into a bowl and add the soy, rice vinegar and the remaining honey and sesame oil. Mix until combined and smooth.

5 Using the unwashed pan, heat the olive oil on the Boiling Plate, and then add the ginger, mushrooms, spring onions, red pepper and mangetout. Cook for about 3–4 minutes, tossing all the time.

6 Stir the sauce into the pan with the vegetables and add the pork and noodles. Toss and season well.

7 Turn into a large bowl, sprinkle with cashew nuts and serve at once.

PREPARE AHEAD
The vegetables can be prepared in advance but it is best cooked to serve.

CONVENTIONAL OVEN
Cook on the hob in the usual way.

Pork Mimosa

The wonderful blend of spices gives a real mellowness to the sauce, which is in no way hot and fiery. Serve with plain boiled rice (see page 150), some mango chutney and a fresh mango, cut into cubes. Creamed coconut comes in packets and is usually found in good supermarkets near the curry powders in the Indian food section.

25g (1 oz) butter
900g (2 lb) pork fillet, cut in 1cm (½ in) slices
1 large Spanish onion, cut in wedges
2 fat garlic cloves, crushed
1 × 2.5cm (1 in) piece of fresh root ginger, peeled and finely chopped
1 level tablespoon each of ground cumin, ground coriander, ground turmeric and medium curry powder
salt and freshly ground black pepper
1 × 400g (14 oz) tin of chopped tomatoes
150ml (5 fl oz) chicken stock or water
50g (2 oz) creamed coconut, cut into pieces
1 × 250g (9 oz) carton of full-fat Greek yoghurt
fresh mint or coriander leaves

1 Melt the butter in a fairly large pan on the Boiling Plate and brown the meat. Lift out with a slotted spoon and put to one side.

2 Add the onion and garlic, stir, cover the pan and transfer to the floor of the Simmering Oven for 10 minutes.

3 Remove the lid, stand the pan on the Boiling Plate, and add the ginger and spices. Season and mix well. Stir in the tomatoes and stock, and bring to the boil, stirring. It will be a thick mixture at this stage. Drop in the meat and coconut, bring back to the boil and simmer for a few minutes.

4 Cover and transfer to the Simmering Oven for about 30 minutes, or until the meat is tender.

5 Before serving, stir in the yoghurt, pour into a dish and garnish with the mint or coriander leaves.

PREPARE AHEAD
Can be made completely up to a day ahead. It can also be frozen for up to 3 months. Before serving, stir in the yoghurt.

CONVENTIONAL OVEN
Cook in an oven preheated to 160°C/Fan 140°C/ Gas 3, for about 1 hour or until the pork is tender.

Kashmir Lamb

Fillet of lamb in a spiced piquant sauce. Sometimes fillet of neck of lamb is hard to come by so use lean shoulder instead. Most of us are trying to avoid using too many animal fats in cooking these days and, with an Aga, food can often be cooked without using any extra fat at all. Trim the surplus from meats before casseroling – the long, slow-cooking process will create succulent chunks of meat in a rich sauce. Serve with rice flavoured with saffron and a green salad with mint. If you like a lot of sauce add 2 cartons (300ml/ ½ pint) of yoghurt.

675g (1 ½ lb) fillet of neck of lamb
2 tablespoons sunflower oil
1 large onion, chopped
2 fat garlic cloves, crushed
1 teaspoon ground turmeric
1 teaspoon ground cumin
1 teaspoon ground coriander
1 teaspoon flour
150ml (¼ pint) chicken stock
salt and freshly ground black pepper
1 × 150ml (¼ pint) carton of unset natural yoghurt
small handful of fresh coriander

1 Cut the fillet into discs the thickness of thick sliced bread. Measure the oil into a large pan and brown the meat on both sides on the Boiling Plate. Lift out with a slotted spoon into a small ovenproof casserole.

2 Fry the onion in the remaining oil in the unwashed pan and add the garlic. Stir in the spices and flour, and then add the stock, stirring all the time. Allow to thicken, season with salt and pepper and then pour over the meat. Bring back to the boil in the casserole and then cover with a lid.

3 Transfer to the floor of the Simmering Oven for about 1 ½ hours, or until the meat is tender. Just before serving, stir in the yoghurt and mix well. Do not reboil. Garnish with fresh coriander and serve with boiled rice (see page 150).

PREPARE AHEAD
You can make the dish completely up to 2 days ahead. It also freezes well. Stir in the yoghurt to serve.

CONVENTIONAL OVEN
Cook in an oven preheated to 160°C/Fan 140°C/Gas 3 for 1 ½ hours until the meat is tender.

Marinated Butterfly Easter Lamb

A boned leg of lamb cooks quicker. Marinating the meat overnight develops the flavours. Serve with couscous and salad.

1 boned leg of lamb,
about 1kg (2 lb 4 oz)
final weight

MARINADE
finely grated zest
and juice of 1 small lime
2.5cm (1 in) fresh ginger,
finely grated
2 red chillies, deseeded
and thinly sliced
3 garlic cloves, crushed
1–2 tablespoons olive oil

1 Place the boned lamb on a board, open out and slice down through the thickest parts and flatten.

2 Mix all the marinade ingredients together and rub into the lamb. Marinate in the fridge overnight.

3 Place the lamb on the grill rack, set in its lowest position in the large roasting tin.

4 Slide the roasting tin on to the lowest set of runners in the Roasting Oven and roast for 30–40 minutes until browned on the outside but still pink in the centre.

5 Cover with foil and rest for 10 minutes before carving.

PREPARE AHEAD
Marinating is done ahead.
Cook to serve.

CONVENTIONAL OVEN
Roast in an oven preheated to 200˚C/Fan 180˚C/Gas 6 for about 30–40 minutes until browned on the outside but still pink in the centre.

MINT SAUCE
Combine about 12 large springs of mint with 3 level teaspoons of caster sugar and 1½ tablespoons water boiled with 3 tablespoons vinegar in a bowl and mix well until thoroughly blended.

REDCURRANT JELLY
Tie redcurrants as picked in muslin and squeeze out the juice with your hands. Measure the quantity of juice and pour into a large pan. For every 600ml (1 pint) juice, add 450g (1 lb) of sugar. Heat the pan gently until the sugar has dissolved then boil for 4–5 minutes or until setting point is reached (see page 9). Pour into small jars. As a variation add chopped mint to the hot jelly after setting point has been reached. This will keep in a cool place for up to 3 months.

Rack of Lamb with Proper Gravy

Rack of lamb is a roast for a special occasion. You may need
to order it from your butcher in advance.

2 fully trimmed French-
style racks of lamb,
chine bone removed
(usually 14 cutlets in
total, 7 in each rack)
olive oil
salt and freshly ground
black pepper
2 teaspoons Dijon
mustard
1 tablespoon chopped
fresh rosemary

GRAVY

1 level tablespoon
plain flour
65ml (2½ fl oz) red wine
300ml (½ pint) chicken
stock
1 teaspoon
Worcestershire sauce
1 teaspoon lemon juice
1 tablespoon redcurrant
jelly
a dash of gravy
browning

1 Rub the lamb with a little olive oil. Season well
and spread with the Dijon mustard and rosemary.

2 Sit the lamb in the small roasting tin, the bone tips
facing downwards and inwards. Roast at the top of
the Roasting Oven for 12–15 minutes for pink lamb,
20 minutes for well done. This will depend on the
thickness of the rack of lamb.

3 Remove from the tin, wrap loosely in foil, and leave
to rest while you make the gravy.

4 Off the heat, blend the flour with the fat and juices
in the tin, using a metal whisk. Pour in the wine and
remaining ingredients, whisk well, then slide on to the
floor of the Roasting Oven for about 5 minutes until
bubbling and slightly thickened. Check the seasoning.

5 Serve two to three cutlets per person with the gravy,
and perhaps Dauphinoise Potatoes (see page 140),
stir-fried young spinach and young carrots.

PREPARE AHEAD
The red wine, Worcestershire
sauce, lemon juice and
redcurrant jelly can all
be added to the stock
ready to make the gravy.

CONVENTIONAL OVEN
Roast in an oven preheated
to 220°C/Fan 200°C/Gas 7
for about 15 minutes for rare,
20 minutes for well done.

Kleftiko

This Greek dish is very easy and is cooked for ages in the Simmering
Oven until the meat falls off the bone. Use six knuckles of lamb
instead of shoulder, if preferred. The juices are thin for this recipe,
so if you like a thicker sauce, thicken with a little cornflour
and keep the lamb warm while this is being done.

1.3–1.8kg (3–4 lb)
  lean shoulder of lamb,
  boned
4 fat garlic cloves,
  cut in spikes
2 large mild onions,
  sliced
salt and freshly ground
  black pepper
juice of 1 lemon
1 tablespoon chopped
  fresh rosemary
1 tablespoon chopped
  fresh thyme
chopped fresh parsley

1 Open out the shoulder of lamb flat and remove
any pockets of fat and excess fat. Make incisions
into the lamb with a sharp pointed knife and slip
a spike of garlic in each hole. Lay the lamb flat in
the roasting tin, skin side down.

2 Slide the tin on to the top set of runners in the
Roasting Oven and brown the meat. It will take
about 30 minutes.

3 Lift out, remove any fat from the roasting tin,
add the onions to the tin, season and add the lemon
juice, rosemary and thyme. Return the lamb to the tin,
skin side up. Place in the Roasting Oven on the top set
of runners and brown. It will take 20 minutes or so.

4 Transfer to a large ovenproof casserole, cover
and bring to the boil, then transfer to the Simmering
Oven for about 3 hours until really tender.

5 Carve and serve with the onions and juices and
a sprinkling of parsley.

PREPARE AHEAD
Complete step 1 and prepare
the vegetables the day before.

CONVENTIONAL OVEN
Brown the meat first in a non-
stick frying pan then cook
slowly in an oven preheated
to 160°C/Fan 140°C/Gas 3
with the other ingredients for
about 3 hours or until tender.

Glazed Loin of Lamb with Sauce Paloise

A very special and modern French cut of lamb, fillet of loin is the eye meat of loin chops and is sometimes called canon of lamb. The paloise sauce can be made ahead, but cannot be reheated because it would split. It can be kept warm, covered, on the back of the Aga, or you can serve it lukewarm. If liked, serve with proper gravy (see page 100).

2 lamb loins, defatted
  and boneless,
  about 450g (1 lb)
  total weight
1–2 tablespoons
  redcurrant jelly
salt and freshly ground
  black pepper

PALOISE SAUCE

1 quantity Hollandaise
  Sauce (see page 50)
1 teaspoon mint sauce
  from a jar
1 teaspoon chopped
  fresh mint

1 Line the small roasting tin with foil. Spread the lamb fillets with the redcurrant jelly, season well and sit the lamb on the foil in the roasting tin.

2 Roast at the top of the Roasting Oven for 10–15 minutes. Turn once during this time to achieve an even glaze. Allow the meat to rest for 5–10 minutes.

3 Meanwhile, make the paloise sauce by mixing the hollandaise sauce, mint sauce and fresh mint. Keep warm on the back of the Aga on a folded tea towel.

4 Carve the lamb into 1cm (½ in) diagonal slices and serve with the paloise sauce.

PREPARE AHEAD
The sauce can be made
an hour in advance.

CONVENTIONAL OVEN
Quickly brown the meat on
both sides in a non-stick frying
pan, spread with redcurrant
jelly, then cook in an oven
preheated to 220°C/Fan
200°C/Gas 7 for about
10–15 minutes.

Glorious Lamb with Red Onions and Peppers

You could also use thick slices from a leg of lamb, half a leg of lamb taken from the knuckle end or, indeed, knuckles of lamb. Knuckles are usually taken from the shoulder of lamb and are often available frozen.

6 lamb shanks
4 fat garlic cloves,
    roughly chopped
2 large red peppers,
    seeded and
    roughly sliced
3 red onions, quartered
1 × 225g (8 oz) tin of
    chopped tomatoes
150ml (¼ pint) red wine
3 tablespoons
    redcurrant jelly
salt and freshly ground
    black pepper
a little dried rosemary
2 tablespoons chopped
    fresh parsley

1 Arrange the shanks in the greased large roasting tin, and slide on to the top set of runners in the Roasting Oven. Brown the joints, turning once. This will take about 30 minutes or so.

2 Lift out the shanks, drain off any fat and transfer the fat to a deep casserole dish, large enough to take the shanks plus vegetables. Add the garlic, peppers, onions, tomatoes and their liquid, wine, redcurrant jelly, salt, pepper and rosemary. Add the shanks and bring to the boil on the Boiling Plate and cover with a lid.

3 Transfer to the Simmering Oven for about 3 hours or until the meat is exceedingly tender and falling off the bone. Check the seasoning of the juices. If there is any fat on the surface, blot off with kitchen paper.

4 Sprinkle parsley over each shank when serving with the vegetables and juices, and some creamy mashed potatoes.

PREPARE AHEAD
The dish can be made a day ahead and also freezes well for up to 1 month.

CONVENTIONAL OVEN
Cook in an oven preheated to 160°C/Fan 140°C/Gas 3 for about 2–2½ hours until tender.

Irish Stew

True Irish stew is made using only lamb, onions and
potatoes, but we like to include carrots, too.

1.5kg (3 lb) scrag and
  middle neck of lamb
2 large onions
225g (8 oz) carrots
450g (1 lb) potatoes
salt and freshly ground
  black pepper
a generous handful of
  chopped parsley

1 Cut the lamb into neat pieces and remove the spinal
cord. Peel and slice the onions, carrots and potatoes.
Arrange alternate layers of meat with layers of each
vegetable, seasoning each layer with salt and pepper.
Finish with a layer of potato, which should be neatly
arranged to give an attractive appearance to the
finished dish. Pour in sufficient water to half fill
the casserole. Cover with a lid.

2 With the grid shelf on the third set of runners
cook in the Roasting Oven for about 15–20 minutes
until boiling.

3 Transfer to the floor of the Simmering Oven
for about 2½ hours.

4 Remove the lid and return to the Roasting Oven for
about 20–30 minutes to brown the potatoes. Sprinkle
with chopped parsley to serve.

PREPARE AHEAD
The dish can be assembled a
day ahead and cooked to serve.
It also freezes well cooked for
up to 2 months.

CONVENTIONAL OVEN
Cover and cook in an oven
preheated to 200°C/Fan
180°C/Gas 6 for about 15–20
minutes until boiling. Reduce
the temperature to 160°C/Fan
140°C/Gas 3 and continue to
cook for about 3 hours. Increase
the heat to 200°C/Fan 180°C/
Gas 6 and remove the lid for
the final 20–30 minutes of
the cooking time in order
to brown the potatoes.

Shepherd's Pie with Potato and Celeriac Mash

A twist on the old classic. If you make it with only mashed celeriac it is a bit too soft so we have added potatoes.

1kg (2¼ lb) lean
  minced lamb
2 onions, chopped
2 medium carrots, peeled
  and finely diced
50g (2 oz) plain flour
150ml (¼ pint) Port
300ml (½ pint) beef stock
1 tablespoon redcurrant
  jelly
1 tablespoon
  Worcestershire sauce
1 tablespoon finely
  chopped fresh
  rosemary
2 fresh bay leaves
salt and freshly ground
  black pepper
a dash of gravy browning
  (optional)
a little melted butter

TOPPING
750g (1 lb 10 oz) peeled
  King Edward potatoes,
  diced
750g (1 lb 10 oz) peeled
  celeriac, diced
a good knob of butter

PREPARE AHEAD
Can be made up to a day ahead.
Freezes well without the mash.

CONVENTIONAL OVEN
Cook the finished dish in an oven preheated to 200°C/Fan 180°C/Gas 6 for about 45 minutes.

1 Grease a 1.7 litre (3 pint) wide ovenproof dish.

2 Heat a large frying pan on the Boiling Plate. Add the lamb and fry, stirring until browned. You may need to drain off a little fat if the mince is fatty.

3 Add the onions and carrots and fry for a few minutes. Sprinkle in the flour and stir. Blend in the Port and stock, stirring all the time, and bring to the boil. Add the redcurrant jelly, Worcestershire sauce, rosemary and bay leaves and stir to combine. Season with salt and pepper and add a dash of gravy browning to give a darker colour. Once boiling, cover with a lid and transfer to the Simmering Oven for an hour.

4 While the mince is cooking, put the potatoes and celeriac in a saucepan, cover with water and add salt. Bring to boil on the Boiling Plate and boil for 5 minutes. Drain the water from the saucepan, cover with a lid and transfer to the Simmering Oven for about 40 minutes or until tender. Tip the celeriac, potato and a little butter into a processor and whiz until smooth. Season to taste and be careful not to overmix.

5 Spoon the mince into the prepared dish, discarding the bay leaves, and leave to cool. Spread the mash over the cold mince and fork the top. Brush with a little melted butter and slide on to the second set of runners in the Roasting Oven for about 40 minutes until golden and bubbling.

Moussaka

Blanching the aubergines instead of frying
them makes the dish lighter and healthier.

900g (2 lb) minced lamb
1 tablespoon
   sunflower oil
2 large onions, chopped
2 fat garlic cloves,
   crushed
40g (1½ oz) flour
150ml (¼ pint) red wine
1 tablespoon tomato
   purée
2 × 400g (14 oz) tins
   of chopped tomatoes
salt and freshly ground
   black pepper
2 teaspoons chopped
   fresh mint
3 small aubergines,
   sliced into 1 cm (½ in)
   slices

SAUCE
50g (2 oz) butter
50g (2 oz) flour
600ml (1 pint) hot milk
grated nutmeg
1 level teaspoon Dijon
   mustard
175g (6 oz) Cheddar
   cheese, grated
1 egg, beaten

1 You will need a large, 1.7 litre (3 pint) shallow ovenproof dish, greased.

2 Put the lamb into a large pan and cook on the Boiling Plate until the fat begins to run out, stir and add oil if necessary. Add the onions and garlic and fry until brown.

3 Sprinkle in the flour and stir until combined. Add the wine and boil for a few minutes to reduce. Stir in the tomato purée, tinned tomatoes, seasoning and mint. Bring to the boil, cover with a lid and transfer to the Simmering Oven for about 45 minutes.

4 Meanwhile, blanch the aubergines in a pan of boiling water for 1 minute. Drain, then dry on kitchen paper.

5 To make the sauce, heat the butter in a pan, add the flour and cook for a minute. Gradually blend in the milk, stirring well and bring to the boil. Add the nutmeg, mustard, seasoning and cheese. Cool slightly then stir in the egg.

6 To assemble the moussaka, put half the meat mixture into the prepared dish and then cover with half the aubergines. Season. Repeat with the remaining lamb and aubergines. Pour over the cheese sauce and slide on to the second set of runners in the Roasting Oven and cook for about 40 minutes until golden and bubbling.

PREPARE AHEAD
The dish can be assembled
up to a day ahead. It also
freezes well uncooked for
up to 2 months.

CONVENTIONAL OVEN
Cook in an oven preheated
to 200°C/Fan 180°C/Gas 6
for about 35–40 minutes
until the top is golden brown.

Beef Wellington

Lucy's absolute favourite and it would be her last supper! We now roast the fillet first before wrapping – this gives a perfect result.

50g (2 oz) butter
1.5kg (3 lb 5 oz) beef fillet, cut from the centre of the fillet
2 large onions, sliced
100g (4 oz) mushrooms, sliced
salt and freshly ground black pepper
1 × 500g (1 lb 2 oz) packet of all-butter puff pastry
beaten egg, to glaze

PREPARE AHEAD

The Wellington can be made completely ahead and chilled in the fridge for up to 24 hours before cooking.

CONVENTIONAL OVEN

Sear the meat on the hob in the usual way. Roast the beef in an oven preheated to 220°C/Fan 200°C/Gas 7 for about 18–20 minutes. Once wrapped in pastry roast for 25–30 minutes and rest for 15 minutes before carving.

TIP

If cooking a larger fillet of beef, say 3kg (6 lb 8 oz), roast for 25–30 minutes and then a further 30–40 minutes in the pastry.

1 Melt the butter in a large frying pan. Brown the whole fillet on all sides until just browned, for about 3–5 minutes. Transfer to a roasting tin.

2 Slide on to the grid shelf on the floor of the Roasting Oven and roast for about 20–22 minutes, turning the meat over once. Lift out on to a plate and cool completely.

3 Add the onions to the juices in the tin and stand on the floor of the Roasting Oven to cook for about 15 minutes or until soft, stirring from time to time. Add the mushrooms and cook for a further 2–4 minutes. Remove from the oven, season and leave to cool. Pour away any excess liquid.

4 Roll out the pastry to a rectangle 35 × 40cm (14 × 16 in) depending on the size of the meat. Place half the mushroom mixture down the centre of the pastry and then place the meat on top, flat side uppermost. Season well. Cut a 3.5cm (1½ in) square from each corner of the pastry for decoration and keep on one side. Brush the edges of the pastry with a little beaten egg and then fold the pastry around the meat, so that it is sealed inside and has no air gaps. Turn over and stand on a baking sheet. Use the leftover pastry to decorate the top with leaves or lattice. Chill in the fridge for 30 minutes. Brush liberally with beaten egg.

5 Roast on the grid shelf on the floor of the Roasting Oven for about 25–30 minutes until pale golden brown. Carve thick slices and serve with gravy made from the reserved mushrooms and onion.

Roast Prime Rib of Beef

Serve with the usual accompaniments – Yorkshire pudding,
roast potatoes and horseradish sauce.

1 × 2-rib joint, either
prime rib cut short,
or wing rib cut short,
about 2.3kg (5 lb)
salt and freshly ground
black pepper
1 large onion, unpeeled
but thickly sliced

GOOD GRAVY

3 tablespoons dripping
1 good tablespoon plain
flour
75ml (2½ fl oz) Port
500ml (18 fl oz) beef
stock
a dash of
Worcestershire sauce
a little gravy browning

PREPARE AHEAD
Best cooked to serve.

CONVENTIONAL OVEN
Roast in an oven preheated
to 220°C/Fan 200°C/Gas 7.
For timings use chart.

1 Sprinkle the beef fat with salt and pepper. Stand
on end in a roasting tin just large enough for the
joint on a bed of thick slices of unpeeled onion
(the onion skin gives colour to the juices). If using
a meat thermometer, insert into the meat in the thickest
part. Transfer to the Roasting Oven and roast as per
the chart below, basting from time to time.

2 When the meat is done, lift out of the tin, loosely
cover with foil and leave to rest in a warm place for
about 20 minutes before carving. Discard the onion,
squeezing any juices into the tin.

3 Meanwhile, make the gravy. Skim off 3 good
tablespoons of fat from the roasting tin. Pour the
rest of the juices into a bowl and put in the fridge
for the fat to rise to the top.

4 Measure the flour into the tin, and whisk with
the 3 reserved tablespoons of fat on the Boiling
Plate. Gradually add the Port and stock, then the
Worcestershire sauce. Remove the fat from the bowl
of juices in the fridge, and add the juices to the gravy,
along with a little gravy browning. Check the seasoning.

5 To carve, slip a sharp knife close to the bone to free
the complete joint, then carve down across the grain.

BEEF	TIME	INTERNAL TEMP
Rare	15 minutes per 450g (1 lb)	60°C
Medium	20 minutes per 450g (1 lb)	70°C
Well done	25 minutes per 450g (1 lb)	75°C

Yorkshire Pudding

100g (4 oz) plain flour
a pinch of salt
3 eggs, beaten
225ml (8 fl oz) milk
a little fat or dripping

PREPARE AHEAD

These reheat extremely well.
Cook the day before, leave
in the tins and allow to cool.
Keep in a cool place overnight.
Reheat in the Roasting Oven
for 10–15 minutes (4-hole tin),
8–10 minutes (12-hole tin), or
15–20 minutes (Aga roasting
tin). They also freeze well.
Cool, then pack and freeze
for up to 2 months.

CONVENTIONAL OVEN

Cook in an oven preheated
to 220°C/Fan 200°C/Gas 7.
For timings, see main recipe.

1 Measure the flour and salt into a bowl. Make a well
in the centre and add the eggs with a little of the milk.
Whisk the eggs and milk together, taking a little flour
from the sides, then whisk in the remaining milk
gradually, drawing in all of the flour to make a smooth
batter. This is best done with an electric hand whisk.

2 Place a little fat or dripping in the bottom of two
4-hole Yorkshire pudding tins, a 12-hole deep patty
tin or the small Aga roasting tin.

3 With the grid shelf on the third set of runners,
heat the tin in the Roasting Oven until the fat has
melted and is very hot. Remove the tin from the oven
and pour in the batter. Return to the oven and cook for
about 20–30 minutes (4-hole tin), 15 minutes (12-hole
tin), 30–40 minutes (Aga roasting tin), or until well
risen and golden brown.

4 Serve at once.

HORSERADISH SAUCE

300ml (½ pint) double cream
4 level tablespoons grated fresh horseradish
2 teaspoons white wine vinegar
salt and freshly ground black pepper
a little caster sugar

1 Lightly whip the cream and add the horseradish.
Stir in the vinegar, salt and pepper. Add a little sugar
to taste and blend thoroughly.

2 Turn into a small serving dish, cover and chill well
before serving.

Salt Beef with Mustard Sauce

Delicious served hot or cold, and great in open sandwiches if you have some left over. You may need to order this from the butcher – ask him to salt the beef a week ahead. If using brisket, remove any excess fat.

1.3kg (3 lb) whole piece
  of salted silverside
  or brisket
450g (1 lb) little whole
  carrots, peeled
450g (1 lb) whole
  shallots, peeled

MUSTARD SAUCE

25g (1 oz) butter
25g (1 oz) flour
150ml (¼ pint) milk
4 teaspoons white
  wine vinegar
2 teaspoons mustard
  powder
2 teaspoons caster sugar
salt and freshly ground
  black pepper

1 Sit the beef in a large saucepan. Cover with cold water and bring to the boil on the Boiling Plate. Cover with a lid and transfer to the Simmering Oven for about 2–2½ hours until tender.

2 Add the carrots and shallots to the pan, bring back to the boil on the Boiling Plate, cover and return to the Simmering Oven for about 30 minutes or until the vegetables are tender.

3 To make the mustard sauce, melt the butter in a small pan on the Boiling Plate. Add the flour and whisk to combine. Gradually add the milk and 150ml (¼ pint) of the beef cooking liquid. Whisk and bring to the boil on the Boiling Plate until thickened. Add the vinegar, mustard and sugar, season with salt and pepper and whisk to combine.

4 Carve thin slices of beef and serve with the vegetables and hot mustard sauce, or serve cold without the sauce.

TIP

This salt beef makes fabulous sandwiches if there are any leftovers. Take slices of fresh bread, e.g. ciabatta, focaccia or baguette, and spread with cream cheese. Lay thin slices of salt beef on top. Add slices of pickled cucumber or gherkin and spoon over a little mustard sauce.

PREPARE AHEAD

Can be made up to 4 days ahead and served cold. The sauce can be made up to 2 days ahead.

CONVENTIONAL OVEN

Bring to the boil and cook on the hob, or cook in an oven preheated to 140°C/Fan 120°C/Gas 2 for 2½ hours.

Beef in Horseradish Cream

This is one of Mary's favourite buffet party dishes and the flavour of the sauce is really different. It can all be prepared well in advance and then the horseradish cream stirred in at the last minute.

900g (2 lb) stewing
  steak
1 tablespoon
  sunflower oil
2 large onions, chopped
1 dessertspoon
  curry powder
1 teaspoon ground
  ginger
1 dessertspoon
  muscovado sugar
40g (1½ oz) flour
450ml (¾ pint) good
  beef stock
2 tablespoons
  Worcestershire sauce
salt and freshly ground
  black pepper
1½ heaped tablespoons
  horseradish cream
a little chopped fresh
  parsley

1 Cut the meat into 2.5cm (1 in) cubes. Heat the oil in a large pan on the Boiling Plate. Add the beef and brown on all sides for a few minutes.

2 Add the onions, curry powder, ginger, sugar and flour to the dish and cook for a minute. Stir in the stock and bring to the boil, stirring until thickened. Add the Worcestershire sauce and seasoning, cover with a lid and simmer for about 5 minutes.

3 Transfer to the floor of the Simmering Oven for about 4 hours until the meat is tender (use the floor grid in an Aga Total Control or City60).

4 When ready to serve, stir in the horseradish cream and turn into a warm serving dish. Sprinkle with parsley and serve at once.

PREPARE AHEAD
The dish can be made up to 2 days ahead. It also freezes well. Stir in the horseradish cream and sprinkle with parsley to serve.

CONVENTIONAL OVEN
Cook in an oven preheated to 160°C/Fan 140°C/Gas 3 for about 4 hours until the meat is tender. Stir in the horseradish cream and sprinkle with parsley to serve.

Steak and Kidney Pudding

We like plenty of gravy, so we cook a little extra kidney and onion
to make a good stock in a small pan in the Simmering Oven.
Then we use this to make more gravy to serve with the pudding.

550g (1¼ lb) skirt
   of beef
175–225g (6–8 oz)
   ox kidney
1 onion, finely chopped
1 level tablespoon flour
1 tablespoon
   Worcestershire sauce
salt and freshly ground
   black pepper
scant 150ml (¼ pint)
   water

SUET CRUST PASTRY
225g (8 oz) self-raising
   flour
100g (4 oz) shredded
   suet
a pinch of salt
about 7–8 tablespoons
   water

1 Grease a 1.4 litre (2½ pint) pudding basin.

2 Cut the steak into 1cm (½ in) cubes, removing any
fat. Trim the core from the kidney and cut into small
even pieces. Put the steak and kidney in a bowl with
the onion, flour, Worcestershire sauce and seasoning.
Mix together well.

3 To make the pastry, put the flour, suet and salt into
a bowl. Gradually add the water and mix to a soft but
not sticky dough. Take a third of the pastry and roll out
on a lightly floured surface to a circle large enough to fit
the top of the basin. Roll out the remaining dough and
use to line the basin.

4 Fill the basin with the meat mixture and then pour
in the water. Dampen the edges of the pastry and cover
with the pastry lid, pressing the edges firmly together
to seal. Cover the pudding with a pleated piece of
greaseproof paper and then a lid of foil. Stand the basin
in a pan and pour in boiling water until it comes
halfway up the sides of the basin. Bring to the boil
and simmer for 30 minutes.

5 Transfer the basin, water and pan to the floor
of the Simmering Oven and cook for about 6 hours
until the meat is tender.

PREPARE AHEAD
The pudding can be made
up to a day ahead and reheated.

CONVENTIONAL OVEN
Either simmer in the pan on
the hob (checking occasionally
on the level of boiling water)
for 2½ hours, or cook in an
oven preheated to 160°C/Fan
140°C/Gas 3 for 6 hours until
the meat is tender.

Steak and Ale Pie

Here's some great pub food without having to walk to the pub.
Do feel free to replace the puff pastry with shortcrust.
Serve with a nice heap of garden vegetables.

2–3 tablespoons
  sunflower oil
500g (1 lb 2 oz) stewing
  steak, cubed
1 large onion, chopped
2 tablespoons flour
1 × 500ml (18 fl oz)
  bottle of local ale
salt and freshly ground
  black pepper
225g (8 oz) button
  mushrooms,
  quartered
280g (10 oz) all-butter
  puff pastry
beaten egg, to glaze

1 You will need 4–6 individual pie dishes or 1 large 1.75 litre (3 pint) pie dish.

2 Measure the oil into a pan. Add the steak and quick fry on the Boiling Plate until browned – you may need to do this in batches. Remove with a slotted spoon and set aside.

3 Tip the onion into the pan and fry for a few minutes. Add the flour, stir and cook for a minute, then slowly stir in the ale. Return the meat to the pan, season and add the mushrooms. Bring to the boil, cover with a lid and transfer to the floor of the Simmering Oven for about 2 hours, or until the meat is tender. Turn into a pie dish and leave to cool.

4 Roll out the pastry to cover the top and then glaze with the beaten egg.

5 Place on the grid shelf on the floor of the Roasting Oven and cook for 20–25 minutes until the pastry is golden brown and the meat heated through.

PREPARE AHEAD
Can be cooked up to a day ahead and reheated.

CONVENTIONAL OVEN
Brown the meat in a non-stick frying pan on the hob, then cook slowly in an oven preheated to 160°C/Fan 140°C/Gas 3 with the other ingredients for about 2 hours or until tender. Assemble the pie, increase the temperature to 220°C/Fan 200°C/Gas 7 and cook for about 20–25 minutes.

Chilli con Carne

Perfect for all the family. If you are feeding teenagers who love chilli, add a bit more! Serve with sour cream and grated Cheddar or red Leicester cheese.

2 tablespoons olive oil
2 large onions, chopped
1 red chilli, deseeded and diced
3 garlic cloves, crushed
900g (2 lb) minced beef
1 tablespoon ground coriander
2 tablespoons ground cumin
2 × 400g (14 oz) tins of chopped tomatoes
1 tablespoon tomato purée
200ml (⅓ pint) beef stock
1 × 400g (14 oz) tin of red kidney beans
salt and freshly ground black pepper

1 Heat the oil in a large pan on the Boiling Plate. Add the onions, chilli and garlic and fry for 2–3 minutes.

2 Add the minced beef and brown on the high heat until golden, stirring. Sprinkle in the spices and fry for another minute. Stir in the tinned tomatoes, purée, stock and beans and season with salt and pepper.

3 Bring to the boil, cover and transfer to the Simmering Oven for about 1–1½ hours or until tender.

4 Serve with rice (see page 150), sour cream and cheese.

PREPARE AHEAD
Can be made up to 2 days ahead and reheated to serve. It also freezes well without the beans.

CONVENTIONAL OVEN
Cook on the hob on a low heat or in an oven preheated to 160°C/Fan 140°C/Gas 3 for about 2 hours.

Calves' Liver with Sage and Lemon

If you like your liver rare, just half a minute on each side is sufficient cooking time. Make sure that your butcher cuts the liver in thin slices whichever way you like it.

450g (1 lb) fresh calves' liver, thinly sliced
salt and freshly ground black pepper
25g (1 oz) butter
3 sprigs of sage, the leaves chopped coarsely, or 1 teaspoon dried sage
juice of ½ a lemon

1 Season the liver on both sides.

2 Melt the butter in a large frying pan on the Boiling Plate, then add the sage.

3 Bring the butter to foaming point and then drop in the slices of liver a few at a time. Fry for barely a minute on each side and then squeeze in the lemon juice. Serve at once with mashed potato, a green veg and the juices from the pan poured over the liver.

PREPARE AHEAD
Best cooked to serve.

CONVENTIONAL OVEN
Cook on the hob in the usual way.

CHAPTER

FOUR

VEGETABLE SIDES

VEGETABLES

Vegetables are so versatile – a nutritious meal in themselves or a delicious accompaniment to a main course, they add enormously to the presentation of food with such a rich choice of colours and different varieties so readily available.

The wonder of the Aga! Just think, baked potatoes for one, two or twenty-two, the heat is always there – use it.

ARTICHOKES

Globe: an attractive, leafy, globe-shaped vegetable. Choose large fresh green ones.

Cut off the stalks, wash well, trim tops off outer leaves, then immerse in boiling water and cook until tender – about 40 minutes on the Simmering Plate. Drain upside down and serve hot or cold. To eat pull off each leaf one by one and dip the fleshy end into melted butter, mayonnaise or French dressing, then scrape off the fleshy part with the teeth. Discard the leaves and when they have all been removed, take away the 'choke' (the hairy bit) and you are left with the 'fond' (fleshy base). This is the best part!

Jerusalem: these are small, off-white, knobbly root vegetables. The flavour is subtle and they are reasonably priced. Buy clean fleshy-looking ones.

Scrub them clean and cook in their skins. They are extremely difficult to peel raw because of their shape. Cook in boiling salted water, covered with a lid, on the Simmering Plate for about 8 minutes. Lift out with a slotted spoon, place in a colander and run under cold water until cool enough to handle. Peel off the skins, slice the artichokes thickly and return to the pan with 3 tablespoons fresh water, cover with the lid and bring to the boil. Transfer the pan to the floor of the Simmering Oven for a further 10 minutes to cook until just tender. Serve with parsley sauce or just melted butter.

ASPARAGUS

A luxury vegetable best very simply served so as not to impair their superb flavour. Select straight, even stalks with compact, closed tips. The thicker the stems, the better the quality; they should look fresh and the tips should be bright green. Best eaten fresh.

Wash the asparagus and trim off the woody ends. Scrape down the stalks. Bring a pan of salted water to the boil on the Boiling Plate and then cook the asparagus immersed in the water until just tender. This will take 4–6 minutes according to the thickness. Drain well. To eat, dip each tip into melted butter; if the stalks are very young almost all of these may be eaten, too.

AUBERGINES

These now come in various colours, the best known is a glossy purple, though they can be mottled purple and white, or smaller and completely white – this is why they are also known as 'egg plants'.

Slice and fry gently in a little oil on the Simmering Plate or use for made up dishes, such as Moussaka or Ratatouille. No need to peel them. Halved aubergines may be scooped out and stuffed with minced meat or chopped vegetables.

BEANS AND PEAS

Green beans, runner beans, broad beans and peas add variety at different times of the year. Choose firm, bright, stiff-looking beans and, in the case of broad beans and peas, those that look well-filled in the pod.

Top and tail green and runner beans and remove the strings. Either leave the green beans whole or cut into 2.5cm (1 in) slices. Slice runner beans diagonally. Shell broad beans and peas. Bring a pan of salted water to the boil on the Boiling Plate and cook until just tender. Green beans take about 6–8 minutes if whole, 3–5 minutes if cut; runner beans about 3–5 minutes; broad beans about 2–3 minutes; fresh peas 2–3 minutes, depending on size. They may all be drained and served with a little butter and freshly ground black pepper. Broad beans can be popped straight from their pods to be served in salads.

BEAN SPROUTS

Small fleshy white shoots with green hoods.

Rinse in cold water and use raw in salads or cook for one minute in a stir-fry.

BEETROOT

At its best pulled young. Good not only cooked but finely shredded raw in salads.

Wash well to remove soil and cut off the stalks to within about 2.5cm (1 in) of the root. Be careful when washing not to damage the skin otherwise the beetroot will 'bleed'. Boil for 10 minutes on the Boiling Plate and transfer to the Simmering Oven in the water for about 2–3 hours, depending on size. Remove the skin after cooking. Serve hot with a white sauce or cold, sliced in vinegar, or in a salad.

BROCCOLI

There are three main kinds of broccoli. The most well-known is **purple sprouting broccoli**, which has several heads of purple/green flower buds and leaves on one stem. **Calabrese** has a large head, usually on one stem. **Cape broccoli** is similar to cauliflower except that the colour is purple and the head more open.

Trim off the ends of the stalks or stalk, and wash. Slice any thick stalks. Bring a pan of salted water to the boil on the Boiling Plate, add the stalks and cook covered with a lid for 2 minutes, add the rest of the broccoli and continue to cook until just tender. Purple sprouting broccoli takes about 5 minutes; calabrese about 6 minutes; cape broccoli about 7 minutes. Drain well, toss in a little butter and serve seasoned with freshly ground black pepper.

BRUSSELS SPROUTS

Good not only cooked but finely shredded raw in salads.

Trim the ends of the sprouts and remove any tatty outside leaves. Cut a cross in the base of the stalk of large sprouts with a sharp knife; this helps them to cook more quickly. Bring a pan of salted water to the boil on the Boiling Plate, enough to almost cover the sprouts, add the vegetables and cook for about 6–8 minutes until just tender – have the lid half on. Drain well and serve tossed in a little melted butter and freshly ground black pepper. Add fried chestnuts or fried almonds to buttered sprouts for a special occasion. If you want them to cook even more quickly, cut them in half before boiling.

CABBAGE

Red, green and white, curly kale and greens – cabbage is usually the cheapest vegetable and I think one of the best.

With green or white cabbage remove any limp, damaged or coarse outer leaves, then quarter and remove the thick stalk. Shred, wash and cook. Bring a large pan with a little salted water to the boil on the Boiling Plate, add the cabbage and cook uncovered for a few minutes, then partially cover the pan for the last few minutes. The total cooking time will be 5–6 minutes depending on the age of the cabbage. When cooked, it should still be crisp. Drain well, toss in butter and lots of freshly ground black pepper. Cook kale and greens in the same way, but shred the leaves and remove any coarse ribs or stems.

CAULIFLOWER

So often cauliflower is overcooked; it is so much more delicious and nutritious when slightly underdone.

Trim off all but a few green leafy branches at the stem. Divide the cauliflower into large florets with a little leaf attached to some. Cook in boiling salted water barely covering the cauliflower, on the Boiling Plate with a tight-fitting lid on the pan. Serve with butter and black pepper, or with a good sauce made with half milk and half cauliflower water.

CELERIAC

An off-white, knobbly-looking, turnip-shaped vegetable, this is root celery. Choose fleshy-looking celeriac, which is heavy for its size.

Peel off the brown skin just before cooking; doing it too soon means it will discolour. This can be prevented by adding a couple of tablespoonfuls of lemon juice to the cooking water. Cube and cook in a pan of boiling salted water on the Simmering Plate, covered with a lid for about 15 minutes until tender, then toss in butter, or cook a little longer, transferring to the Simmering Oven and mash to a purée. If liked it may be mixed with an equal quantity of mashed potato, adding salt and black pepper. For salads: cut into julienne strips, blanch for a few moments, allow to cool, then toss in mayonnaise.

CHICORY

Use when the chicory is young and firm, before the leaves yellow.

Remove outside leaves if necessary, trim the root end and wash. Place in a buttered Aga casserole and cover with good chicken stock and the juice of ½ a lemon, then season. Bring to the boil and simmer on the Simmering Plate for 10 minutes, and then transfer to the Simmering Oven for about 45 minutes to 1 hour.

CORN ON THE COB

A beautiful-looking vegetable with a subtle flavour. Choose ears of corn that are well filled and pale yellow – the deep golden ones are over-ripe.

Remove any leaves and threads, and trim the stalk. Cook in boiling water on the Boiling Plate until tender for about 10 minutes. Drain, toss in butter and eat with fingers, or speared on corn picks.

COURGETTES (ZUCCHINI)

Very delicious, they should be bright green, shiny and heavy for their size.

Wipe, slice if liked or leave whole, trimming away each end. Cook in boiling salted water on the Boiling Plate until just tender. Whole will take about 5 minutes; sliced about 2 minutes. Drain well, return to the pan and toss in butter with black pepper. They can also be sliced and fried gently on the Simmering Plate in a little butter for about 15 minutes until tender.

FLORENCE FENNEL

Can be served raw in salad but is more often cooked. It has a mild aniseed flavour.

Trim any leafy stems and the root. Cut into quarters, boil in salted water, with a little lemon juice, on the Boiling Plate for 5 minutes. Drain and replace the lid, then transfer to the Simmering Oven for 45 minutes. Serve covered with white sauce or au gratin.

LEEKS

Useful to serve in winter soups, casseroles or for adding to meat pies.

First, remove just the very end of the root with a sharp knife, the tops of the leaves and any damaged leaves. If serving them sliced, wash in several lots of water and drain. If cooking them whole, cut through to within 5cm (2 in) of the base three times and soak in warm water for 10 minutes, then rub the leeks with the hands under running cold water until all the earth is washed away. The cooking time very much depends on the thickness of the stalk. Boil in salted water on the Boiling Plate until tender. Sliced leeks should take about 5 minutes; whole leeks about 10 minutes. Drain very well and serve with a little white sauce or just butter and freshly ground black pepper.

MANGETOUT AND SUGAR SNAP PEAS

Choose crisp flat pods.

Top and tail, string if necessary. Boil rapidly on the Boiling Plate in 2.5cm (1 in) salted water until tender, about 3–5 minutes. Drain and serve with a knob of butter and freshly ground black pepper.

MARROW

Choose younger smaller marrows if cooking as a vegetable. The larger ones are good when stuffed and baked.

Peel, cut in half and remove the seeds. Cut in slices or cubes, and cook in boiling salted water on the Boiling Plate for 3–5 minutes until just tender, drain thoroughly. Serve in a white sauce or with butter and black pepper.

MUSHROOMS

Do not peel, wash if large, wipe if small, dry on kitchen paper, trim stalks. Fry gently in butter on the Simmering Plate or use in stews, casseroles and sauces.

OKRA (LADIES' FINGERS)

A green podded vegetable which looks like a pointed ridged bean. Choose firm, plump green pods.

Cook in a little boiling salted water on the Boiling Plate for about 5 minutes until just tender, then drain and toss in butter. If overcooked they tend to turn slimy. They are also good stir-fried.

PEPPERS

These now come in many colours – green, red, yellow, purple and white. Remove stalk and scoop out core and seeds. Use cooked in savoury dishes, stuffed whole, or sliced in salads.

PULSES

Dried seeds of plants such as beans and peas.

Generally these should be left to soak overnight before cooking. To cook, pour off the water and cover with fresh water, adding a bouquet garni for extra flavour. Bring to the boil on the Boiling Plate, simmer for 10 minutes and then transfer to the Simmering Oven until tender, about 1–3 hours, depending on the type.

N.B. Boil red kidney beans for 15 minutes before simmering.

UNDERGROUND VEGETABLES

The well-known ones – potatoes, carrots, parsnips, kohlrabi, turnips and swedes. Wonderful cooked in the Simmering Oven – no steam in the kitchen.

For old potatoes, carrots, parsnips and turnips, use a potato peeler and remove any eyes or small blemishes. The first new potatoes, or small ones, are best just scrubbed. All can be kept, peeled in cold water until needed (the convenience may outweigh the loss of vitamins). If they are needed for the weekend, do them on Friday, change the water on Saturday and keep them very cold. Swedes need peeling with a vegetable knife. Bring a pan of salted water to the boil on the Boiling Plate. I use about 2 teaspoons of salt to each 600ml (1 pint) water. Add vegetables and cook with the lid on for about 5 minutes. Drain off all the water, replace the lid and transfer to the floor of the Simmering Oven for about 30 minutes–1 hour or until just tender. Root vegetables will keep beautifully in the Simmering Oven like this for up to 2 hours. To serve, add butter and season with freshly ground black pepper. For mashed potatoes, add milk, too.

N.B. The cooking time in the Simmering Oven depends on the size of vegetable.

A Collection of Chef's Vegetables

All the vegetables are cooked to perfection ahead, even the day before!
Keep the vegetables covered in a cool place until they are needed,
then blast with heat in the Roasting Oven until piping hot, but
not re-cooked. Vary the vegetables as you wish.

about 900g (2 lb) baby
   new potatoes, washed
salt and freshly ground
   black pepper
about 225g (8 oz)
   prepared leeks, washed
   and thinly sliced
about 225g (8 oz) young
   green beans, trimmed
about 225g (8 oz) new
   whole baby carrots,
   trimmed
about 225g (8 oz)
   broccoli florets
a little melted butter

PREPARE AHEAD

Prepare up to a day ahead
to the end of step 6.

CONVENTIONAL OVEN

Cook the vegetables on the hob
in the usual way, as indicated
to the end of step 6, then cook
in an oven preheated to 220°C/
Fan 200°C/Gas 7, for about
25–30 minutes until the
vegetables are piping hot.

TIP

Don't attempt to keep the
vegetables hot: they will
lose their perfect colour
and crispness.

1 Bring the potatoes to the boil in salted water on
the Boiling Plate, cover and simmer for 2 minutes.
Drain, cover with a lid and transfer to the floor of
the Simmering Oven for about 30 minutes or until
just tender. Refresh in cold water, drain well.

2 Add the leeks to fresh boiling salted water as
above and cook for about 2 minutes, then remove
from the water with a slotted spoon. Refresh in
cold water, then drain well on kitchen paper.

3 Add the beans to the same boiling water and cook
as above for about 4–5 minutes until al dente. Remove
from the water, refresh with cold water, then drain
well on kitchen paper.

4 Add the carrots to the same boiling water and cook
as above for about 5 minutes until just tender. Remove
from the water, refresh in cold water, then drain well
on kitchen paper.

5 Add the broccoli florets to the same boiling water
and cook as above for about 2–3 minutes until just
tender. Remove from the water, refresh in cold
water, then drain well on kitchen paper.

6 Toss each batch of vegetables, individually, in a
smidgen of melted butter and season well. Arrange
in a large flat ovenproof dish, and cover tightly
with buttered foil.

7 Place the dish on the floor of the Roasting Oven
for about 20 minutes until the vegetables are steaming
and you can hear the butter sizzle. Serve at once.

Baked Fennel with Red Peppers and Parmesan

This combination of Mediterranean vegetables
goes well with steak and lamb.

3 heads of fennel
salt and freshly ground
  black pepper
½ red pepper, deseeded
  and cut into
  pencil-thin strips
1–2 tablespoons
  olive oil
50–75g (2–3 oz)
  Parmesan cheese,
  coarsely grated
a little paprika

1 Remove the tops of the fennel and cut each bulb into four wedges. Cook in boiling salted water on the Boiling Plate for about 10 minutes, then drain and refresh in cold water.

2 Toss the fennel and strips of pepper in the olive oil until all are coated well.

3 Arrange the fennel quarters in an ovenproof dish, placing strips of pepper in between. Season with salt and pepper, sprinkle with the Parmesan, and dust with paprika.

4 Bake on the floor of the Roasting Oven for 15–20 minutes until the fennel is tender.

PREPARE AHEAD
Prepare up to the end of step 3. Cover and keep in the fridge for up to 12 hours before baking.

CONVENTIONAL OVEN
Cook in an oven preheated to 200°C/Fan 180°C/Gas 6 for 20–25 minutes until the fennel is tender.

Roasted Mediterranean Vegetables

Alter the vegetables as you like – fennel and red onions work well, too. This dish is very good with lamb. If you want to serve the vegetables cold in summer with salad, add a little balsamic vinegar.

2 large onions
2 yellow peppers, deseeded
2 red peppers, deseeded
4 medium courgettes
1 large aubergine
2 fat garlic cloves
3 tablespoons olive oil
salt and freshly ground black pepper

1 First prepare the vegetables. Quarter the onions, cut the peppers into large pieces, thickly slice the courgettes and cut the aubergine into 2.5cm (1 in) chunks. Crush the garlic.

2 Toss the onion in 1 tablespoon of the olive oil in a polythene bag, sprinkle with salt and pepper and turn out into the large roasting tin. Put on the floor of the Roasting Oven for about 20 minutes until beginning to soften and brown.

3 Toss the rest of the prepared vegetables and the garlic with the remaining oil in the same polythene bag and then add to the onions in the tin. Return to the floor of the Roasting Oven for about 20–30 minutes until the vegetables are tender and well browned. Turn the vegetables over occasionally with a wooden spatula to ensure they brown evenly.

PREPARE AHEAD
Complete to the end of step 3, but undercook the vegetables slightly. Cool, cover and keep in the fridge for up to a day ahead.

CONVENTIONAL OVEN
Cook in an oven preheated to 230°C/Fan 210°C/Gas 8 for about 30–40 minutes, cooking the onion first for about 10 minutes.

Baked Potatoes

Lucy likes to cut the potatoes in half before baking. It cuts down the baking time by at least a third and the cut side has a crisp brown appearance.

4 large potatoes
oil
25–50g (1–2 oz) butter,
   for serving

PREPARE AHEAD
Best cooked to serve.

CONVENTIONAL OVEN
Cook in an oven preheated
to 220°C/Fan 200°C/Gas 7
for about 1¼ hours. The time
will vary depending on the
size of the potatoes.

1 Scrub the potatoes thoroughly and prick with a fork. Brush with oil, if liked.

2 With the grid shelf on the third set of runners, bake the potatoes in the Roasting Oven for about 1¼ hours. The time will vary depending on the size of the potatoes.

3 Cut each potato in half, fork up the inside slightly and serve dotted with butter.

Lucy's Mash

A classic potato dish cooked the Aga way.

900g (2 lb) potatoes,
   peeled and cubed
3 tablespoons hot milk
butter
salt and freshly ground
   black pepper

PREPARE AHEAD
Best cooked to serve.

CONVENTIONAL OVEN
Cook on the hob in the
usual way.

1 Boil the potatoes on the Boiling Plate for about 5 minutes. Drain, cover with the lid and transfer to the Simmering Oven for about 40 minutes.

2 Mash the potato with the milk, butter and seasoning and serve.

VARIATIONS
Add 2 tablespoons chopped fresh chives or parsley
Add 2 teaspoons grainy mustard
Add 1 tablespoon mango chutney
Add 2 teaspoons mint sauce and 2 teaspoons fresh chopped mint

Rösti

Take care not to boil the potatoes for too long; they should still be very firm which makes the grating easier.

900g (2 lb) large
   potatoes, scrubbed
salt and freshly ground
   black pepper
50g (2 oz) pork dripping
   or goose fat

PREPARE AHEAD

Can be made up to 6 hours ahead.

CONVENTIONAL OVEN

Roast in an oven preheated to 220°C/Fan 200°C/Gas 7 for about 25 minutes until golden brown.

1 Boil the potatoes in salted water on the Simmering Plate for 10 minutes or until the point of a knife can be inserted into the potato for about 2.5cm (1 in) before meeting resistance. Drain, cool and peel the potatoes.

2 Grate the potatoes coarsely into a bowl, add seasoning and mix well.

3 With the grid shelf on the floor of the Roasting Oven, melt half the dripping or butter in a small roasting tin. Add the grated potato, flattening it with a fish slice. Dot with the remaining dripping or butter and return to the oven for about 25 minutes until golden brown.

Roast Potatoes

If you need to roast the potatoes quickly, cut them into smaller pieces.

900g (2 lb) medium potatoes
goose fat, lard, oil or dripping

PREPARE AHEAD

Roast the potatoes for only 20–30 minutes. Remove excess fat from the tin and allow the potatoes to cool. When needed, re-roast in the Roasting Oven for about 20 minutes.

CONVENTIONAL OVEN

Cook in an oven preheated to 220°C/Fan 200°C/Gas 7 for about an hour.

1 Peel the potatoes and cut into even-sized pieces. Parboil in salted water for 5–8 minutes, or until nearly tender, on the Boiling Plate then drain well, using a colander. Shake the colander to fluff up the edges of the potatoes.

2 Place a good knob of fat or a little oil in a small roasting tin. Place the tin on the floor of the Roasting Oven until the fat or oil is sizzling.

3 Add the potatoes and return to the floor of the Roasting Oven for about 1–1¼ hours, turning often, or until the potatoes are crisp and golden brown.

Dauphinoise Potatoes

A wonderful way to serve up potatoes that can be prepared ahead and reheated to serve. Traditionally dauphinoise potatoes are made with all cream, which is delicious but rather rich. If this is how you like them, add 450ml (15 fl oz) double cream instead of the stock and cream.

melted butter
1.3kg (3 lb) old potatoes, washed
salt and freshly ground black pepper
1 garlic clove, crushed
225ml (8 fl oz) chicken stock, or water and 1 chicken stock cube
225ml (8 fl oz) double pouring cream
a little chopped fresh parsley

1 Line the base and sides of a small roasting tin with greaseproof or non-stick baking paper, and brush generously with melted butter.

2 Peel and thinly slice the potatoes. Arrange the slices in the roasting tin, seasoning between the layers. Blend the crushed garlic with the stock and cream, and pour some in between the layers and some over the top.

3 Bake on the lowest set of runners in the Roasting Oven, covered with buttered paper, for about 45 minutes. Turn around halfway through the cooking time. When the potatoes are tender, remove the buttered paper and return to the top of the Roasting Oven for 12 minutes until golden brown. Scatter with chopped parsley to serve.

PREPARE AHEAD
The dish can be assembled up to 6 hours ahead.

CONVENTIONAL OVEN
Cook the potatoes in the roasting tin in an oven preheated to 200°C/Fan 180°C/Gas 6 for about 1 hour. Remove the buttered paper and return to the oven for about 15 minutes until golden brown.

Carrot and Swede Purée

A colourful vegetable dish, so easily cooked in the Simmering Oven.
This method works equally well replacing the swede and carrot
with celeriac and potato, or parsnip and potato.

450g (1 lb) swede,
  peeled and sliced
450g (1 lb) carrots,
  peeled and sliced
salt and freshly ground
  black pepper
generous knob
  of butter

1 Put the swede and carrots into a large pan, cover
with salted water and bring to the boil on the Boiling
Plate. Cover and transfer to the Simmering Plate
for 5 minutes.

2 Drain and replace the lid. Transfer to the floor
of the Simmering Oven for about an hour or until
tender. Season and mash with a generous amount
of butter, or reduce to a purée in a processor.

3 Turn into a warm dish to serve.

PREPARE AHEAD
Can be made up to 6
hours ahead.

CONVENTIONAL OVEN
Cook on the hob in the
usual way.

Cauliflower, Squash and Broccoli Cheese

Great combination and colour, too.

1 large cauliflower
  (about 500g/1 lb 2 oz)
salt
350g (12 oz) butternut
  squash, peeled and cut
  into very small dice
350g (12 oz) broccoli,
  broken into small
  florets
a little paprika

CHEESE SAUCE

50g (2 oz) butter
50g (2 oz) flour
600ml (1 pint) hot milk
100g (4 oz) well-
  flavoured Cheddar
  cheese, grated
75g (3 oz) Guyère
  cheese, grated
freshly ground
  black pepper
1 tablespoon Dijon
  mustard

1 Grease a 1.7 litre (3 pint) wide ovenproof dish.

2 Divide the cauliflower into florets, discarding any leaves and very thick stalk.

3 Bring a pan of water to a rolling boil on the Boiling Plate. Add some salt and the squash cubes and boil for 2 minutes. Add the cauliflower, bring back to the boil and boil for 1 minute. Finally, add the broccoli, bring back to boil and boil for 2 minutes. Drain and run under cold water to stop cooking. Arrange all the vegetables in the prepared dish.

4 To make the sauce, heat the butter in a pan on the Boiling Plate until melted, then whisk in the flour and cook for a minute. Gradually blend in the milk and bring to the boil, stirring until thickened. Add two-thirds of each cheese and season with pepper and mustard.

5 Pour the sauce over the vegetables, sprinkle with the remaining cheeses and dust with paprika. Cook on the second set of runners in the Roasting Oven for about 20–25 minutes until golden and bubbling around the edges.

PREPARE AHEAD
Can be prepared up to a day ahead and cooked to serve.

CONVENTIONAL OVEN
Cook in an oven preheated to 200°C/Fan 180°C/Gas 6 for about 20–25 minutes.

Tomato and Herb Bulgar Wheat Salad

Good colour with lots of herbs. We have used bulgar wheat
but you could use couscous if preferred; cook in the same
way. You could also replace the mint with basil.

225g (8oz) bulgar wheat
350ml (12 fl oz)
    vegetable stock
1 good teaspoon
    Dijon mustard
1 teaspoon honey
juice of 1 lemon
4 tablespoons olive oil
6 spring onions, sliced
½ cucumber, peeled,
    deseeded and diced
4 tomatoes, skinned,
    deseeded and diced
4 tablespoons chopped
    fresh mint
4 tablespoons chopped
    fresh parsley
salt and freshly ground
    black pepper

1 Measure the bulgar wheat into a small saucepan and
pour in the stock. Bring to the boil on the Boiling Plate,
cover and transfer to the Simmering Oven for about
15 minutes or until the liquid has been absorbed and
the wheat is tender. Tip into a large bowl.

2 Mix the mustard, honey, lemon juice and oil together
in a bowl, and whisk to combine. Add to the wheat and
leave to cool.

3 Add all the remaining ingredients, season with salt
and pepper and toss together.

PREPARE AHEAD
Can be made up to a day ahead
but add the dressing, cucumber
and tomato up to 2 hours
before serving.

CONVENTIONAL OVEN
Follow the packet instructions
and cook on the hob in the
usual way.

Seed and Nut Munchies

These are so moreish, you will go back for more and more!
Perfect nibbles to go with drinks.

Makes 450g (1 lb)
50g (2 oz) sesame seeds
100g (4 oz) pumpkin
    seeds
100g (4 oz) blanched
    whole almonds
100g (4 oz) cashew nuts
100g (4 oz) sunflower
    seeds
1 tablespoon olive oil
2 teaspoons soy sauce
2 teaspoons runny
    honey
salt and freshly ground
    black pepper

1 Measure all the seeds and nuts into a small Aga
roasting tin. Pour over the oil and toss.

2 Slide on to the grid shelf on the floor of the
Roasting Oven for about 10 minutes, stirring
from time to time until lightly golden.

3 Add the soy and honey to the nuts and mix well.
Season and return to the floor of the Roasting
Oven for 3–4 minutes until golden.

4 Serve with drinks as a snack or scatter over salads.

PREPARE AHEAD
Can be made up to
4 days ahead.

CONVENTIONAL OVEN
Cook in an oven preheated
to 200°C/Fan 180°C/Gas 6
as above.

PASTA
AND
RICE

Cooking Rice

A faultless way of oven cooking rice using the absorption method.
Be exact with quantities and every grain of rice will be separate.

225g (8 oz) basmati rice
350ml (12 fl oz) water
    or
225g (8 oz) brown rice
420ml (14 fl oz) water
    or
275g (10 oz) easy-cook
    long-grain rice
50g (2 oz) wild rice
450ml (15 fl oz) water

1 Wash the rice and measure into a 2 litre (3½ pint) pan with the water and 1 teaspoon of salt. Bring to the boil on the Boiling Plate.

2 Stir, replace the lid and put on the floor of the Simmering Oven for about 15–20 minutes (basmati, easy-cook long-grain, wild rice) or 40–45 minutes (brown), until the liquid is absorbed and the rice is tender.

PREPARE AHEAD
Best cooked to serve.

CONVENTIONAL OVEN
Cook on the hob in the usual way.

3 tablespoons good
    olive oil
2 teaspoons medium
    curry powder
about 3 sweet red
    onions (175g/6 oz),
    thinly sliced
1 garlic clove, crushed
1 aubergine, cut
    into cubes
1 red pepper, deseeded
    and sliced
1½ tablespoons
    soy sauce
salt and freshly ground
    black pepper
1½ tablespoons chopped
    fresh parsley

VARIATION
FRAGRANT RICE

1 Cook rice as directed above. Meanwhile, heat the oil in a generous-sized pan, add the curry powder, onions and garlic and cook on the Boiling Plate for 2–3 minutes. Add the aubergine and red pepper and cook for a further 3 minutes. Cover and transfer to the floor of the Simmering Oven for 10 minutes until tender.

2 Return the pan of vegetables to the Boiling Plate and boil off any excess juices. Stir in the cooked rice, add the soy and season well. Scatter with the parsley before serving.

Pilau Rice

We like a crispy top to the rice so after making it on the hob
we cook it in the oven. You can serve the rice before cooking
in the oven for the final time if preferred.

75g (3 oz) frozen
　petit pois
salt and freshly ground
　black pepper
225g (8 oz) easy-cook
　long-grain or
　basmati rice
2 tablespoons olive oil
1 large onion, chopped
1 red pepper, deseeded
　and diced
3 garlic cloves, crushed
250g (9 oz) button
　mushrooms, sliced
1 teaspoon cumin
　powder
1 teaspoon coriander
　powder
50g (2 oz) butter
juice of ½ a small lemon

1 You will need a 1.2 litre (2 pint) ovenproof
dish, buttered.

2 Cook the peas in boiling salted water for 4 minutes,
drain and refresh in cold water and set aside.

3 Measure the rice into a saucepan, add 450ml (16 fl oz)
water, a pinch of salt and bring to the boil on the
Boiling Plate. Once boiling, cover with a lid and
transfer to the Simmering Oven for 15–20 minutes
or until the water has been absorbed and the rice is
cooked and fluffy.

4 Meanwhile, heat a frying pan on the Boiling Plate,
add the oil, onion and red pepper and fry for a minute.
Cover with a lid and transfer to the Simmering Oven
for 15 minutes or until tender.

5 Return the onion to the Boiling Plate, add the garlic
and mushrooms and fry for a couple more minutes.
Sprinkle in the spices, then add the butter, cooked rice
and peas, and toss. Season with salt and pepper and
stir in the lemon juice.

6 Spoon into the prepared dish and slide on to the
second set of runners in the Roasting Oven for
20–30 minutes or until golden and crispy.

PREPARE AHEAD
Can be prepared to step 6
up to 8 hours ahead.

CONVENTIONAL OVEN
Cook on the hob in the usual
way. Finish the dish in an
oven preheated to 200°C/Fan
180°C/Gas 6 for 20 minutes.

Roasted Garlic and Mushroom Risotto

An intense flavour of garlic with mushrooms, broccoli and leeks.

1 small garlic bulb
(about 8 cloves)
olive oil
a knob of butter
2 small leeks, sliced
225g (8 oz) Arborio
risotto rice
150ml (¼ pint)
white wine
600ml (1 pint)
chicken stock
300g (10½ oz) chestnut
mushrooms, sliced
75g (3 oz) Parmesan
cheese, grated
salt and freshly ground
black pepper
200g (7 oz) long
tenderstem
broccoli spears

1 Slice the garlic bulb in half and sit it on some foil on a small baking sheet. Drizzle with a little oil and roast on the second set of runners in the Roasting Oven for about 20 minutes or until soft and golden. Set aside to cool.

2 Melt a knob of butter in a frying pan on the Boiling Plate, add the leeks and fry for a minute. Stir in the rice and cook for a further minute. Pour in the wine and stock, cover and bring to the boil. Transfer to the Simmering Oven for about 20 minutes until the liquid has absorbed but the rice still has a little bite.

3 Meanwhile, squeeze the roasted garlic cloves out of the bulb and mash the pulp. Heat another knob of butter in a frying pan on the Boiling Plate and fry the mushrooms for a few minutes until browned.

4 Stir the garlic, mushrooms and Parmesan into the risotto and season.

5 Slice the stems of the broccoli into rounds and leave the florets in small pieces. Boil in salted water on the Boiling Plate for about 3–4 minutes or until just tender. Add the broccoli to the risotto and a splash of the cooking water if a little thick. Serve immediately.

PREPARE AHEAD
Best cooked to serve.

CONVENTIONAL OVEN
Cook on the hob in the usual way.

Nasi Goreng

A Malaysian dish that we love. You could also
add cooked prawns on top, if you like.

300g (10 oz) easy-cook
    long-grain rice
salt and freshly ground
    black pepper
olive oil
1 large onion, chopped
500g (1 lb 2 oz) minced
    pork
3 garlic cloves, crushed
1 small red chilli,
    deseeded and finely
    chopped
2 teaspoons medium
    curry powder
4 tablespoons dark
    soy sauce
2 tablespoons sweet
    chilli sauce
2 chicken breasts, sliced
    into thin strips
125g (4½ oz) frozen
    petit pois, cooked
    according to packet
    instructions
6 eggs
prawn crackers, to serve

PREPARE AHEAD

The dish can be made
a day ahead. Cook the
chicken and peas on the day.

CONVENTIONAL OVEN

Cook the rice and the chicken
on the hob in the usual way.
Cook the finished dish in an
oven preheated to 200°C/Fan
180°C/Gas 6 for 30 minutes.

1 You will need a large, shallow, 1.7–2 litre (3–3 ½ pint)
ovenproof dish.

2 To cook the rice, measure it into a pan, cover with
450ml (¾ pint) water, add a teaspoon of salt and bring
to the boil. Cover and transfer to the Simmering Oven
for about 20 minutes or until fluffy and the liquid has
been absorbed. Set aside to cool.

3 Meanwhile, heat 2 tablespoons of olive oil in a large
frying pan on the Boiling Plate. Add the onion and fry
for 2 minutes. Add the pork and brown quickly. Add the
garlic, chilli and curry powder and toss. Stir in the soy
and 1 tablespoon of the chilli sauce. Finally, add the
cooked rice, toss together and season with salt and
pepper. Tip into the ovenproof dish and slide on to
the second set of runners in the Roasting Oven for
30 minutes, turning halfway through.

4 Meanwhile, season the chicken strips and coat in
the remaining chilli sauce. Heat a little oil in a frying
pan on the Boiling Plate, add the chicken and fry for
a few minutes until golden and cooked through.

5 Scatter the chicken and peas on to the rice, toss
a little, and then return to the oven for a further
10 minutes.

6 When you are ready to serve, fry the eggs on the
Simmering Plate (see page 4). Place a fried egg on
top of each serving and offer prawn crackers and
chilli dipping sauce on the side.

Crispy Baked Penne with Bacon and Mushrooms

A family favourite and great to prepare ahead.

250g (9 oz) penne pasta
2 large onions, roughly
   chopped
250g (9 oz) streaky
   bacon, snipped
   into small pieces
250g (9 oz) chestnut
   mushrooms,
   thickly sliced
a knob of butter
250g (9 oz) baby
   spinach
100ml (3½ fl oz)
   double cream
150g (5 oz) mozzarella
   cheese, cubed

SAUCE

50g (2 oz) butter
50g (2 oz) plain flour
600ml (1 pint) hot milk
juice of ½ a lemon
1 tablespoon Dijon
   mustard
100g (4 oz) Parmesan
   cheese, grated
salt and freshly
   ground pepper

PREPARE AHEAD

Can be completed up to
the end of step 6 a day ahead.

CONVENTIONAL OVEN

Bake in an oven preheated
to 200°C/Fan 180°/Gas 6
for 40 minutes.

1 Butter a 2 litre (3½ pint) shallow ovenproof dish.

2 Measure the pasta and onions into a pan of boiling salted water and boil on the Boiling Plate until the pasta is just cooked. Drain and refresh in cold water. Leave in the colander.

3 Scatter the bacon over a small roasting tin, slide on to the grid shelf on the floor of the Roasting Oven and cook for about 10 minutes. Add the mushrooms and a knob of butter, toss around and return to the floor of the Roasting Oven for a further 5 minutes. Remove and set aside.

4 Meanwhile, boil the kettle and pour the boiling water over the spinach in a colander so that it wilts. Leave to cool then squeeze out all the water.

5 To make the sauce, melt the butter in a large pan on the Boiling Plate. When melted, add the flour and whisk to form a roux. Gradually add the hot milk, bring to the boil, whisking until thickened. Add the lemon juice, mustard and half the Parmesan. Season with salt and pepper and whisk until smooth.

6 Add the pasta, mushrooms, bacon and spinach to the sauce and stir well. Tip into the prepared dish and level the top.

7 Pour over the cream and scatter over the mozzarella cheese and the remaining Parmesan.

8 Bake in the middle of the Roasting Oven for 30–40 minutes until bubbling and golden brown.

Smoked Salmon Tagliatelle

These quantities will serve 4 as a main course or 6 as a starter.
A quick note on pasta – all my pasta recipes give cooking times
for dried pasta. If you're using fresh pasta, the cooking time is much
shorter. Smoked salmon has a strong flavour so very little is needed.

225g (8 oz) tagliatelle
a good knob of butter
150ml (¼ pint)
   double cream
100g (4 oz) smoked
   salmon, cut into fine
   strips
juice of ½ a lemon
salt and freshly ground
   black pepper
1 tablespoon chopped
   fresh dill
1 tablespoon chopped
   fresh parsley

1 Cook the pasta until just tender. Drain well and leave in the colander.

2 Add the butter to a large non-stick pan and allow to melt on the Simmering Plate.

3 Return the pasta to the pan with half the cream, the smoked salmon, lemon juice and seasoning to taste. Heat gently until warmed through. Add the remaining cream and half the herbs.

4 Serve in a large bowl or platter and sprinkle with the remaining herbs.

TIP

When entertaining, and you're short of time (or money), never be afraid to serve the simplest food. So long as it is cooked properly, and is of the best quality, it will be appreciated. A salad can be served as a starter instead of accompanying the main course, and a couple of good cheeses or a bowl of fresh fruit can be the perfect end to a meal.

PREPARE AHEAD
Best cooked to serve.

CONVENTIONAL OVEN
Cook on the hob in the usual way.

Spaghetti Bolognaise

Classic and delicious. Cook in the Simmering Oven rather than on the top plates to prevent the Aga losing heat. Always bring to the boil on the top first. If cooking for children, substitute stock for the wine.

2 tablespoons olive oil
250g (9 oz) smoked
    streaky bacon,
    chopped
2 onions, finely chopped
2 carrots, peeled and
    finely chopped
2 garlic cloves, crushed
1kg (2¼ lb) lean minced
    beef
200ml (⅓ pint) red wine
2 × 400g (14 oz) tins
    of chopped tomatoes
2 tablespoons tomato
    purée
2 bay leaves
1 tablespoon chopped
    fresh rosemary
½ teaspoon sugar
salt and freshly ground
    black pepper

1 Heat the oil in a large deep frying pan on the Boiling Plate. Add the bacon, onions and carrots and fry for about 3 minutes until starting to soften. Add the garlic and minced beef. Cook, frying and stirring, until brown all over.

2 Pour in the wine and bring to the boil. Add the remaining ingredients and boil for a few minutes, stirring. Cover and transfer to the Simmering Oven for about 1–1½ hours or until tender.

3 Check the seasoning and serve with cooked spaghetti and grated Parmesan cheese.

PREPARE AHEAD

Can be made up to 3 days ahead and reheated. The Bolognaise freezes well once cooked.

CONVENTIONAL OVEN

Cook over a low heat on the hob in the usual way.

Beef Lasagne

A firm family favourite – best made ahead so the lasagne softens.
If cooking for children, substitute stock for the wine. Be careful
not to overlap the sheets when layering. This lasagne has a lot
of sauce which makes it quite loose – if you prefer a firmer
lasagne add an extra layer of pasta.

1 tablespoon olive oil
2 onions, roughly
chopped
6 rashers bacon,
chopped
3 garlic cloves, crushed
675g (1½ lb) lean
minced beef
2 level tablespoons flour
2 × 400g (14 oz) tins
of chopped tomatoes
100ml (3½ fl oz) red
wine
2 tablespoons tomato
purée
a dash of sugar
1 tablespoon chopped
fresh thyme
salt and freshly ground
black pepper
9 sheets of lasagne

CHEESE SAUCE
50g (2 oz) butter
50g (2 oz) plain flour
600ml (1 pint) hot milk
100ml (3½ fl oz)
double cream
1 tablespoon Dijon
mustard
100g (4 oz) Gruyère
cheese, grated

1 Grease a deep 2.3 litre (4 pint) ovenproof dish.

2 Heat the oil in a deep frying pan on the Boiling Plate.
Add the onions, bacon and garlic and fry for 2 minutes.
Stir in the mince and brown on the heat. Add the
flour and cook for a further minute. Stir in the tinned
tomatoes, wine, purée, sugar and thyme. Season well,
stir until boiling, then cover and transfer to the
Simmering Oven for 1 hour until tender.

3 Meanwhile, to make the cheese sauce, melt the butter
in a saucepan on the Simmering Plate. Add the flour
and stir for a few seconds. Whisk in the hot milk and
cream and stir until thickened. Add the mustard and
half of the cheese. Season well.

4 Put a quarter of the mince in the base of the dish.
Cover with a quarter of the cheese sauce then arrange
three sheets of lasagne on top. Repeat until you have
three layers of pasta and four layers of sauces. Sprinkle
with the remaining cheese.

5 Bake on the grid sheet on the floor of the Roasting
Oven for about 35–40 minutes until golden brown
and the pasta is cooked through. Serve piping hot
with dressed salad leaves.

PREPARE AHEAD
Can be completed to the end
of step 4 up to a day ahead
and cooked as above from
room temperature to serve.
Can be frozen for up to 1 month.

CONVENTIONAL OVEN
Cook in an oven preheated
to 200°C/Fan 180°/Gas 6
for 40 minutes.

Veggie Lasagne with Mushrooms and Tomato

Our favourite vegetable lasagne, full of flavour
and with a classic white sauce.

2 tablespoons olive oil
1 onion, chopped
400g (14 oz) button
    mushrooms, sliced
2 garlic cloves, crushed
2 × 400g (14 oz) tins
of chopped tomatoes
1 tablespoon chopped
    fresh thyme
2 teaspoons balsamic
    vinegar
a dash of sugar
2 tablespoons sun-dried
    tomato paste
500g (1 lb 2 oz) baby
    spinach, trimmed
salt and freshly ground
    black pepper
6–8 sheets lasagne

CHEESE SAUCE

50g (2 oz) butter
50g (2 oz) flour
600ml (1 pint) hot milk
1 tablespoon Dijon
    mustard
250g (9 oz) Gruyère
    cheese, grated

1 You will need a 1.8 litre (3 pint) capacity ovenproof dish.

2 Heat the oil in a large frying pan on the Boiling Plate. Add the onion and fry for a few minutes. Add the mushrooms and garlic and fry for 2 minutes, stirring. Add the tinned tomatoes, thyme, vinegar, sugar, tomato paste and spinach and fry for a further 5 minutes, until the spinach has wilted and the sauce is bubbling. Season with salt and pepper.

3 To make the cheese sauce, melt the butter in a pan on the Boiling Plate. Add the flour and stir for a minute. Whisk in the milk, add the mustard and half of the cheese. Season and bring to the boil, whisking for a few minutes to thicken.

4 Put a third of the vegetables in the base of the ovenproof dish. Spread a third of the cheese sauce over the top and then finish with half of the lasagne sheets. Continue until you have three layers of vegetables and cheese sauce and two layers of pasta. Sprinkle with the remaining cheese.

5 Slide on to the third set of runners in the Roasting Oven for about 30–35 minutes or until golden brown, bubbling around the edges and the pasta is tender.

TIP

If using dried pasta, I make this ahead in the morning or even the day before – this gives time for the sauces to soften the pasta before cooking.

PREPARE AHEAD

Can be made to the end of step 4 up to a day ahead. It also freezes well for up to 1 month.

CONVENTIONAL OVEN

Cook in an oven preheated to 200°C/Fan 180°C/Gas 6 for about 30–35 minutes or until golden brown.

AFTERNOON TEA

THE AGA CAKE BAKER
AND 2-OVEN AGAS

Large round cakes requiring more than
45 minutes cooking can be baked in the
Roasting Oven of the 2-oven Aga using
the special Aga Cake Baker. Other foods
that need a high temperature, such as
scones or bread rolls, can be cooked at
the same time.

We have not used the Aga Cake Baker
in this book as not everyone has one.
If you decide not to use your Aga Cake
Baker, or you don't have one, it is possible
to bake such cakes in a 2-oven Aga, but
they need more attention:

Put the grill rack into the large roasting
tin, place the cake on the rack and slide
the tin into the Roasting Oven, on the
lowest set of runners. Put the cold plain
shelf on the second set of runners. Bake
until the cake is an even, golden brown
on top, usually in about 20–30 minutes.
Check just before 20 minutes.

Transfer the exceedingly hot plain
shelf from the Roasting Oven to the
centre of the Simmering Oven, then very
carefully lift the cake on to the hot plain
shelf and continue to bake until cooked –
usually about 1 hour 30 minutes,
depending on the cake. To test when the
cake is done, take a fine skewer and insert
it into the centre of the cake. If it comes
out clean then the cake is cooked.

N.B. If the Aga is not up to full
temperature, say after a long cooking
session, leave the cake longer in the
Roasting Oven until it is golden, but less
time in the Simmering Oven, just until
a skewer comes out clean when pierced
into the centre of the cake and the cake
is shrinking away slightly from the
sides of the tin.

Lemon Drizzle Traybake

Everyone's favourite, this is Mary's signature cake and one we have been making for years. Traybakes work brilliantly in the Aga as you can use your Aga roasting tins.

225g (8 oz) butter,
  softened, or
  baking spread
225g (8 oz) caster sugar
275g (10 oz) self-raising
  flour
1 level teaspoon
  baking powder
4 eggs
4 tablespoons milk
finely grated rind
  of 2 lemons

FOR THE TOPPING
175g (6 oz) granulated
  sugar
juice of 2 lemons

1 You will need a small Aga roasting tin greased and lined with baking parchment.

2 Measure all the traybake ingredients into a large bowl and beat for about 2 minutes until well blended and smooth. Turn into the prepared tin and level the top.

3 Bake on the grid shelf on the floor of the Baking Oven for 25 minutes or until the cake has shrunk from the sides of the tin and springs back when pressed in the centre with your fingertips. Leave to cool in the tin for a few minutes, then turn out, carefully peel off the parchment and finish cooling on a wire rack. Stand the wire rack on a tray to catch any drops of the topping.

2 oven Bake on the grid shelf on the floor of the Roasting Oven with the cold plain shelf on the second set of runners for about 20–25 minutes.

4 While the cake is baking make the topping. Mix the sugar and lemon juice together in a bowl and stir to a runny consistency. Brush or spoon the lemon topping over the cake while it is still warm and leave to set.

LARGE AGA ROASTING TIN
To make in the large roasting tin, double the quantities and cook for 30–35 minutes.

PREPARE AHEAD
Can be made up to 2 days ahead and kept in an airtight tin. It also freezes well for up to 1 month.

CONVENTIONAL OVEN
You will need a greased and lined 30 × 23cm (12 × 9 in) traybake tin. Bake in an oven preheated to 160°C/Fan 140°C/ Gas 3 for 35–40 minutes.

Too-Good-To-Miss Carrot Traybake

Not just carrots, but bananas and walnuts as well!

225g (8 oz) self-raising flour

2 level teaspoons baking powder

150g (5 oz) light muscovado sugar

100g (4 oz) carrots, coarsely grated

2 ripe bananas, mashed

2 eggs

150ml (5 fl oz) sunflower oil

50g (2 oz) shelled walnuts, chopped

TOPPING

225g (8 oz) full-fat cream cheese

75g (3 oz) butter, softened

175g (6 oz) icing sugar, sifted

a little vanilla extract

1 Line the small roasting tin with foil and grease it well. Measure all the traybake ingredients except the walnuts into a bowl. Beat well with a wooden spoon or with an electric beater until smooth, then fold in the nuts. Pour into the tin.

2 Bake on the grid shelf on the floor of the Baking Oven for about 30–40 minutes, until pale golden and shrinking away from the sides of the tin. If the top is getting too brown after 25 minutes, slide the cold plain shelf above on the second set of runners.

2 oven Bake on the grid shelf on the floor of the Roasting Oven, with the cold plain shelf on the second set of runners above, for about 30–40 minutes, turning once after 25 minutes.

3 Cool. Turn out on to a tray or board and remove the foil.

4 Measure the ingredients for the topping into a mixer, and mix until smooth. Spread over the cake, swirling with a spatula. Chill before serving and cut into pieces.

LARGE AGA ROASTING TIN

To make in the large roasting tin, double the quantities and cook for 40–50 minutes.

PREPARE AHEAD

Weigh out ingredients earlier in the day, and line the tin. Wrap the un-iced traybake in foil and freeze for up to 2 months.

CONVENTIONAL OVEN

You will need a greased and lined 30 × 23cm (12 × 9 in) traybake tin. Bake in an oven preheated to 180°C/Fan 160°C/Gas 4 for about 45 minutes, until the cake is golden brown and firm to the touch. Make the icing as in step 4.

Chocolate Fudge Traybake

Who can resist a chocolate traybake?

40g (1½ oz) cocoa
    powder
65ml (2½ fl oz)
    boiling water
3 eggs
175g (6 oz) butter,
    softened, or
    baking spread
175g (6 oz) caster sugar
200g (7 oz) self-raising
    flour
2 level teaspoons
    baking powder
2 tablespoons apricot
    jam, warmed

FUDGE ICING
40g (1½ oz) butter
40g (1½ oz) cocoa,
    sieved
250g (9 oz) icing
    sugar, sieved
3½ tablespoons milk

PREPARE AHEAD
Can be made up to 2 days
ahead. Freezes well un-iced.

CONVENTIONAL OVEN
You will need a greased and
lined 30 × 23cm (12 × 9 in)
traybake tin. Bake in an oven
preheated to 180°C/Fan
160°C/Gas 4 for about
25–30 minutes.

LARGE AGA ROASTING TIN
To make in the large roasting
tin, double the quantities and
cook for 35 minutes.

1 You will need the small Aga roasting tin lined with greased baking parchment.

2 Measure the cocoa into a large bowl, add the boiling water and mix to a paste. Add all the remaining ingredients, except the jam, and beat well with a wooden spoon or with an electric beater for about 2 minutes until blended and smooth. Turn into the prepared tin and level the top.

3 Bake on the grid shelf on the floor of the Baking Oven for 20–25 minutes. When the cake is done, the sides should be shrinking away from the tin and the top of the cake will spring back when lightly pressed with a finger. Leave to cool in the tin.

2 oven Bake for 20–25 minutes on the grid shelf on the floor of the Roasting Oven with the cold plain shelf on the second set of runners.

4 While the cake is baking, make the fudge icing. Measure the butter into a pan and heat on the Boiling Plate until melted. Add the cocoa and stir for a few seconds. Remove from the heat and stir in the icing sugar and milk. Beat until smooth – the mixture will look very thick but keep on beating and the icing will become smooth and a perfect spreading consistency.

5 Spread a thin layer of warm jam over the cooled cake, then cover with fudge icing.

Coffee and Walnut Traybake with Crunchy Topping

Coffee walnut is one of our favourite flavours. No special coffee is needed, just your usual instant.

1 tablespoon instant coffee
1 tablespoon boiling water
4 eggs
225g (8 oz) butter, softened, or baking spread
225g (8 oz) self-raising flour
225g (8 oz) caster sugar
1 level teaspoon baking powder

TOPPING

100g (4 oz) walnut pieces
25g (1 oz) light muscovado sugar
1 tablespoon instant coffee
1 tablespoon boiling water

1 You will need a small Aga roasting tin greased and lined with baking parchment.

2 Measure the coffee into a large mixing bowl, add the boiling water and mix until dissolved. Add the remaining traybake ingredients and beat well with a wooden spoon or with an electric beater for about 2 minutes until blended and smooth.

3 To make the topping, tip the walnuts into a processor and whiz until finely ground. Turn into a bowl and mix with the muscovado sugar. Dissolve the coffee in the boiling water and add to the walnut mixture.

4 Turn the cake mixture into the tin and spread out evenly. Sprinkle over the chopped walnut mixture.

5 Bake on the lowest set of runners in the Baking Oven for about 35 minutes or until springy to the touch. You may need to turn halfway through and if it is getting too brown slide in the cold plain shelf.

2 oven Bake on the lowest set of runners in the Roasting Oven with the cold plain shelf on the second set of runners for 30–35 minutes or until springy to the touch. You may need to turn halfway through.

6 Leave in the tin to cool and then cut into pieces.

LARGE AGA ROASTING TIN

To make in the large roasting tin, double the quantities and cook for 40–45 minutes.

PREPARE AHEAD

Can be made up to 2 days ahead. Freezes well.

CONVENTIONAL OVEN

You will need a greased and lined 30 × 23cm (12 × 9 in) traybake tin. Bake in an oven preheated to 180°C/Fan 160°C/Gas 4 for about 35–40 minutes.

Victoria Sandwich

It's safe to say that you can trust your Aga with any kind of cake – from simple baking like our favourite traybakes, to large fruit cakes and celebration cakes. With the all-in-one method the whole process of making this delicious cake takes less than half an hour.

225g (8 oz) butter, softened, or baking spread
225g (8 oz) caster sugar
225g (8 oz) self-raising flour
1 teaspoon baking powder
4 large eggs
4 tablespoons strawberry or raspberry jam
150ml (¼ pint) double cream, whipped
a little caster sugar, for dusting

1 Grease two 20cm (8 in) sandwich tins and line the base of each tin with greased baking parchment.

2 Measure the butter, sugar, flour, baking powder and eggs into a large bowl. Beat well with a wooden spoon or with an electric beater for 2 minutes until smooth and blended. Divide the mixture between the two tins and level the tops.

3 With the grid shelf on the floor of the Baking Oven cook for about 25–30 minutes, until well risen and golden brown.

2 oven With the grid shelf on the floor of the Roasting Oven and the cold plain shelf on the second set of runners, bake in the oven for about 25–30 minutes until well risen and golden brown.

4 Leave to cool in the tins for a few moments, then turn out, peel off the parchment and finish cooling on a wire rack.

5 Once completely cool, spread one cake with jam and, using a palette knife, spread the cream over the jam – right to the edges. Sandwich the other cake on top and then dust with caster sugar to serve.

PREPARE AHEAD
The unfilled cake will keep for 2 days in an airtight container. It also freezes well – fill to serve.

CONVENTIONAL OVEN
Bake in an oven preheated to 180°C/Fan 160°C/Gas 4 for about 25 minutes or until the cake is well risen and golden brown.

VARIATIONS

CHOCOLATE SANDWICH

Blend 2 rounded tablespoons of cocoa with 6 tablespoons of hot water in a bowl and then add the remaining ingredients. Fill the cake with buttercream (blend 100g/4 oz soft butter with 225g/8 oz sieved icing sugar) instead of jam and cream, dust the top with caster sugar and grated chocolate.

ORANGE AND LEMON SANDWICH

Add the finely grated rind of 1 orange or 1 lemon to the cake mixture. Fill with 3 tablespoons of lemon curd mixed with cream or, if preferred, orange- or lemon-flavoured buttercream (see left).

COFFEE SANDWICH

Dissolve 2 heaped teaspoons of instant coffee in a little boiling water and add with the other ingredients. Fill the cake with coffee-flavoured buttercream (add 1 tablespoon of coffee essence to the buttercream – see far left) and dredge with icing sugar.

Little and Large Fairy Cakes

Add decoration to these little cakes as you wish – sweets, chocolate
shapes, sprinkles, grated citrus zest, a dusting of cocoa or cinnamon.
It might also be nice to turn them into butterfly cakes, or colour
the icing with natural colouring and use pretty cases.

100g (4 oz) butter,
  softened, or baking
  spread
150g (5 oz) caster sugar
150g (5 oz) self-raising
  flour
2 large eggs
3 tablespoons milk
½ teaspoon vanilla
  extract

ICING

75g (3 oz) butter,
  softened
175g (6 oz) icing sugar
2 tablespoons milk

1 Make the little cakes in an 18-hole tin, or the large
cakes in a 12-hole muffin tin. Line with paper cases.

2 Measure all the ingredients into a bowl and beat
together well with a wooden spoon or with an electric
whisk until smooth. Spoon into the paper cases.

3 Bake on the grid shelf on the floor of the Roasting
Oven with the cold plain shelf on the second set
of runners for 15–18 minutes (large cakes) or
12–15 minutes (little cakes) until risen and golden.

4 Remove from the oven and leave to cool on a
wire rack.

5 Measure all the icing ingredients into a bowl and
beat together well with a wooden spoon or with an
electric whisk until light and fluffy. Put the icing in
a piping bag with a rose nozzle and pipe some icing
on top of each cake.

Continued overleaf

PREPARE AHEAD
The cakes can be made and
iced up to 4 hours ahead. They
also freeze well un-iced for
up to 2 months.

CONVENTIONAL OVEN
Bake in an oven preheated
to 200°C/Fan 180°C/Gas 6
for about 15–18 minutes
(large cakes) or 12–15 minutes
(little cakes), or until risen
and golden.

Recipe continued

VARIATIONS

CHOCOLATE

Add 150g (5 oz) melted chocolate and 2 tablespoons cocoa powder to the cake mixture. Bake as above. Add 75g (3 oz) melted milk chocolate to the icing and ice as above.

CARROT, GINGER AND CINNAMON

Add 1 teaspoon ground ginger, 1 teaspoon ground cinnamon and 1 coarsely grated carrot to the cake mixture. Bake and ice as above.

FRUITY

Add 50g (2 oz) chopped dried apricots and 50g (2 oz) sultanas to the cake mixture, and sprinkle with demerara sugar before baking. Bake as above. No icing.

LEMON AND ORANGE BUTTERFLY CAKES

Add the finely grated rind of ½ a lemon and ½ an orange to the cake mixture and bake as above to make 12 large cakes. Once cool, slice off the top and cut the sponge disc in half to supply the wings. Add the finely grated rind of ½ a lemon and ½ an orange to the icing and, using a piping bag with a rose nozzle, pipe the mixture into the centre of each cake. Place the wings on top and sprinkle with icing sugar.

Cherry Cake

A classic cake. Washing and drying the cherries thoroughly so that all the moisture is removed helps to prevent them sinking to the bottom of the bake.

175g (6 oz) glacé cherries
225g (8 oz) self-raising flour
175g (6 oz) butter, softened, or baking spread
175g (6 oz) caster sugar
finely grated rind of 1 lemon
50g (2 oz) ground almonds
3 large eggs

DECORATION
150g (5 oz) icing sugar
juice of ½ a lemon
50g (2 oz) chopped almonds
3 glacé cherries

1 Well grease a 20cm (8 in) deep cake tin and line with greased baking parchment.

2 Cut the cherries into quarters, put in a sieve and rinse under running water. Drain well and dry thoroughly on kitchen paper.

3 Measure all the remaining ingredients in a large bowl and beat well with a wooden spoon or with an electric beater for 1 minute to mix thoroughly, then lightly fold in the cherries. The mixture will be fairly stiff, which will help keep the cherries evenly suspended in the cake while it is baking. Turn into the prepared tin and level the top.

4 Slide the cake on to the grid shelf on the floor of the Baking Oven and cook for 20–30 minutes, or until a light brown colour. Slide the cold plain shelf on to the second set of runners and continue to bake for a further 30–40 minutes or until well risen and shrinking away from the sides of the tin. If a skewer inserted into the centre comes out clean, the cake is done.

2 oven Slide the cake on to the grid shelf on the floor of the Roasting Oven with the cold plain shelf on the second set of runners and bake for about 25 minutes until just golden brown. Transfer the (now hot) cold plain shelf to the centre of the Simmering Oven and sit the cake on top. Bake for a further hour or until well risen and shrinking away from the sides of the tin.

Continued overleaf

Recipe continued

5 Leave to cool in the tin for 10 minutes then turn out and finish cooling on a wire rack.

6 To make the decoration, sieve the icing sugar into a bowl and mix with the lemon juice. Stir to a fairly thick icing. Spoon into a piping bag fitted with a tiny plain nozzle, or a bag snipped at the point. Pipe in swirls all over the top of the cake. Pipe a slightly thicker line around the top edge of the cake and press the chopped almonds on to the thicker line to give a nut border around the top. Arrange the 3 cherries in the centre.

PREPARE AHEAD
This cake can be made up to 3 days ahead. Freezes well for up to 3 months.

CONVENTIONAL OVEN
Bake in an oven preheated to 160°C/Fan 140°C/Gas 3 for about 1 hour 20 minutes or until a skewer inserted into the centre comes out clean.

Aga Celebration Fruit Cake

Baking the cake slowly in the Simmering Oven gives excellent results. Bake two tiers of a wedding cake at one time but check first that the tins will go in the oven!

ROUND TIN	18cm (7 in) round	20cm (8 in) round	23cm (9 in) round	25cm (10 in) round	28cm (11 in) round	30cm (12 in) round	33cm (13 in) round
SQUARE TIN	15cm (6 in) square	18cm (7 in) square	20cm (8 in) square	23cm (9 in) square	25cm (10 in) square	28cm (11 in) square	30cm (12 in) square
RAISINS	50g (2 oz)	100g (4 oz)	175g (6 oz)	225g (8 oz)	275g (10 oz)	350g (12 oz)	400g (14 oz)
GLACÉ CHERRIES	100g (4 oz)	225g (8 oz)	350g (12 oz)	450g (1 lb)	550g (1 lb 4 oz)	675g (1 lb 8 oz)	800g (1 lb 12 oz)
CURRANTS	175g (6 oz)	350g (12 oz)	500g (1 lb 2 oz)	675g (1 lb 8 oz)	850g (1 lb 14 oz)	900g (2 lb 4 oz)	1.25kg (2 lb 10 oz)
SULTANAS	100g (4 oz)	225g (8 oz)	350g (12 oz)	450g (1 lb)	550g (1 lb 4 oz)	675g (1 lb 8 oz)	800g (1 lb 12 oz)
SHERRY	2.5 fl oz	¼ pint	¼ pint	½ pint	½ pint	¾ pint	¾ pint
ORANGE RIND	1	1	2	2	2	3	3
BUTTER, SOFTENED	100g (4 oz)	175g (6 oz)	250g (9 oz)	350g (12 oz)	425g (15 oz)	500g (1 lb 2 oz)	575g (1 lb 5 oz)
DARK BROWN SUGAR	100g (4 oz)	175g (6 oz)	250g (9 oz)	350g (12 oz)	425g (15 oz)	500g (1 lb 2 oz)	575g (1 lb 5 oz)
EGGS	2	3	5	6	7	9	10
BLACK TREACLE	½ tablespoon	1 tablespoon	1 tablespoon	2 tablespoons	2 tablespoons	3 tablespoons	3 tablespoons
BLANCHED CHOPPED ALMONDS	25g (1 oz)	50g (2 oz)	75g (3 oz)	100g (4 oz)	150g (5 oz)	175g (6 oz)	200g (7 oz)
SELF-RAISING FLOUR	50g (2 oz)	50g (2 oz)	75g (3 oz)	100g (4 oz)	150g (5 oz)	175g (6 oz)	200g (7 oz)
PLAIN FLOUR	50g (2 oz)	100g (4 oz)	175g (6 oz)	225g (8 oz)	275g (10 oz)	350g (12 oz)	400g (14 oz)
GROUND MIXED SPICE	½ teaspoon	1 teaspoon	1½ teaspoons	2 teaspoons	2½ teaspoons	3 teaspoons	3½ teaspoons
BAKING TIMES	4–8 hours	4–10 hours	4½–11 hours	4½–12 hours	5–13 hours	5½–14 hours	5½–15 hours

The cake can be prepared and left overnight, ready to bake the next day. This is a very moist cake so it keeps well in a cool place for up to 6 months. It also freezes well for up to 6 months.

CONVENTIONAL OVEN

Bake in an oven preheated to 140°C/Fan 120°C/Gas 1. For timings see chart – depending on the size of the tin use the shortest option. For example, for an 18cm (7 in) round tin, cook for 4 hours, or until a skewer inserted into the centre comes out clean, and the cake is firm to the touch.

TIP

If cooking a larger cake in an Aga Total Control, it is recommended that you use the Roasting or Baking Oven on Slumber Mode for the best results when cooking overnight.

1 First prepare the fruit. Chop the raisins with a damp knife and quarter the cherries. Put the fruit in a container and pour over the sherry and stir in the grated rind. Cover with a lid and leave to soak for 3 days, stirring daily.

2 Grease the appropriate-sized tin and line the base and sides with a double layer of baking parchment.

3 Measure the butter, sugar, eggs, treacle and chopped almonds into a large bowl and beat well with a wooden spoon or with an electric beater. Add the flours and spice and mix thoroughly until blended. Stir in the soaked fruit and sherry. Spoon the mixture into the tin and level out evenly.

4 Place the cake tin on the grid shelf (or a rack) on the floor of the Simmering Oven. The cooking time required will be between the minimum and maximum times shown in the table. The times do vary as sometimes older Aga cookers have slower Simmering Ovens – look at the cake after the minimum time shown to gauge further cooking time.

Alternatively, start the cake in the Roasting Oven on the grid shelf on the floor with the cold plain shelf above for about 30 minutes, or until the cake is pale golden. Then transfer the hot plain shelf to the middle of the Simmering Oven and gently transfer the cake on to the hot plain shelf.

5 To check when the cake is done, take a fine skewer and insert it into the centre of the cake. If it comes out clean then the cake is cooked. If not, cook for a further 30 minutes or so. Leave to cool in the tin.

Norfolk Fruit Cake with Ginger

This cake is really moist and packed with fruits, including apricots and cherries. It is a good fruit cake even without the ginger. Simply increase the other fruits to make up the weight if you have no ginger in the store-cupboard.

450g (1 lb) mixed fruits and nuts, such as apricots, roughly chopped; cherries, quartered; shelled nuts, roughly chopped; raisins; sultanas

100g (4 oz) butter, softened, or baking spread

1 teaspoon bicarbonate of soda

175g (6 oz) light muscovado sugar

225ml (8 fl oz) water

2 eggs, beaten

275g (10 oz) self-raising wholemeal flour

2 teaspoons ground ginger

100–175g (4–6 oz) stem ginger, drained of syrup, roughly chopped

1 Grease a 20cm (8 in) deep round cake tin, then line the base with greased baking parchment.

2 Measure the prepared fruits and nuts, butter, bicarbonate of soda, sugar and water into a large pan. Bring up to the boil on the Boiling Plate, and boil for 3 minutes.

3 Allow to cool, then add the eggs, flour, ground ginger and stem ginger. Mix to combine thoroughly then turn into the prepared cake tin and level the top.

4 Put the cake on the grid shelf on the floor of the Baking Oven for about 1¼ hours. Check after 30 minutes, and if the top is getting too brown, slide the cold plain shelf on to the second set of runners from above to prevent it from browning more.

2 oven Sit the grill rack in a large Aga roasting tin and place the cake tin on top. Bake on the lowest set of runners in the Roasting Oven with the cold shelf on the second set of runners for about 30–40 minutes until golden brown on top. Transfer the tin and cake to the Simmering Oven for about an hour, or until a warm skewer inserted into the centre comes out clean.

5 Cool in the tin before turning out on to a rack.

PREPARE AHEAD

This cake keeps well for up to 2 months in a cool place as it is so moist. The cake will also freeze for up to 3 months.

CONVENTIONAL OVEN

Bake in an oven preheated to 160°C/Fan 140°C/Gas 3 for 1¼–1½ hours or until a skewer inserted into the centre comes out clean.

Easter Simnel Cake

This has become the traditional Easter Cake but originally it was given by servant girls to their mothers when they went home on Mothering Sunday.

225g (8 oz) butter, softened, or baking spread
225g (8 oz) light muscovado sugar
4 eggs
225g (8 oz) self-raising flour
225g (8 oz) sultanas
100g (4 oz) currants
100g (4 oz) glacé cherries, washed and quartered
50g (2 oz) candied peel, chopped
grated rind of 2 lemons
2 level teaspoons ground mixed spice

FILLING AND TOPPING
450g (1 lb) almond paste or marzipan
about 2 tablespoons apricot jam
1 egg, beaten, to glaze
crystallised primroses or small eggs

1 Grease a 20cm (8 in) deep round cake tin and line the base with greased baking parchment.

2 Measure all the cake ingredients into a large mixing bowl and beat well with a wooden spoon or with an electric beater until thoroughly blended. Place half of the mixture into the prepared tin and level the surface.

3 Take one-third of the almond paste and roll it out to a circle the size of the tin and then place on top of the cake mixture. Spoon the remaining cake mixture on top and level the surface.

4 Bake on the grid shelf in the centre of the Simmering Oven for 5–10 hours, or until a warm skewer comes out clean from the centre and the cake is pale golden. If the top is getting too brown, cover with a piece of foil.

5 Allow the cake to cool in the tin for about 30 minutes before turning out, peeling off the parchment and cooling on a wire rack.

6 When the cake is cool, brush the top with a little warmed apricot jam and roll out half the remaining almond paste to fit the top. Press firmly on to the cake and crimp the edges to decorate. Mark a criss-cross pattern on the almond paste with a sharp knife. Form the remaining almond paste into eleven balls to represent the Apostles.

7 Brush the almond paste with the beaten egg and arrange the almond paste balls around the outside. Brush the tops of the balls with beaten egg, too, and then wrap all but the top of the cake in foil. Stand in a roasting tin and slide the tin into the centre of the Roasting Oven. Brown for a few minutes until the balls are golden.

8 To decorate fill the centre of the top of the cake with crystallised primroses or small foil eggs.

PREPARE AHEAD
This cake keeps well undecorated in a cool place for up to 2 months. It also freezes well undecorated for up to 3 months.

CONVENTIONAL OVEN
Bake in an oven preheated to 150°C/Fan 130°C/Gas 2 for about 2½ hours or until well risen, evenly brown and firm to the touch. Use a hot grill to turn the almond paste golden.

Classic Swiss Roll

We use self-raising flour, although we were taught to use plain.
We find we get success every time with no effort. It is essential
to weigh the ingredients accurately for this recipe.

SPONGE

4 large eggs, at room
    temperature
100g (4 oz) caster sugar
100g (4 oz) self-raising
    flour
1 teaspoon vanilla
    extract

FILLING

150ml (¼ pint) double
    cream
4 tablespoons raspberry
    or strawberry jam

PREPARE AHEAD

Can be filled and rolled up
to 2 hours ahead and kept in
the fridge. It also freezes well
filled and rolled.

CONVENTIONAL OVEN

Bake in an oven preheated
to 200°C/Fan 180°C/Gas 6,
for about 10 minutes or until
the sponge is golden brown
and begins to shrink from
the edges of the tin.

TIP

If you warm the caster sugar
this will help the eggs whisk
quicker and give more bulk
to the sponge.

1 Grease a 30 × 23cm (12 × 9 in) Swiss roll tin and
line with baking parchment.

2 Whisk the eggs and sugar together in a large bowl
or freestanding mixer until the mixture is light and
frothy and the whisk leaves a trail when lifted out.

3 Gently sieve in the flour and add the vanilla extract,
carefully folding into the mixture with a metal spoon
(do not beat otherwise this will knock out the air).
Pour the mixture into the tin and give it a gentle shake,
or smooth with the back of a spoon, so that the mixture
finds its own level and is spread evenly into the corners.

4 Bake on the grid shelf on the floor of the Roasting
Oven with the cold sheet on the second set of runners
for about 12 minutes until golden brown, firm and
springing away from the sides of the tin.

5 Leave to cool for 5 minutes on a wire rack. While
the cake is cooling, cut out a piece of baking parchment
a little bigger than the tin and sprinkle it with caster
sugar. Invert the cake on to the sugared paper. Quickly
loosen the parchment on the bottom of the cake and
peel it off.

6 To make rolling easier, score a 2cm (¾ in) line along
one short end of the Swiss roll, being careful not to cut
right through. Tightly roll up the Swiss roll using the
paper and leaving the paper inside. Leave to cool.

7 Whisk the cream until soft peaks. Carefully unroll the
sponge, remove the paper and spread the jam over the
sponge. Top with a layer of cream and reroll tightly.
Cut into slices to serve.

VARIATIONS

COFFEE AND WALNUT SWISS ROLL

4 large eggs, at room temperature
100g (4 oz) caster sugar
100g (4 oz) self-raising flour
3 tablespoons instant coffee
300ml (½ pint) double cream
4 tablespoons icing sugar
25g (1 oz) walnut pieces, roughly chopped

1 Make the sponge as above (steps 1–3) but do not put the mixture in the tin.

2 Dissolve the coffee in 3 tablespoons of boiling water. Add half of this to the sponge mixture and carefully fold in. Bake, cool and roll as above.

3 Whisk the cream until soft peaks then fold in the sugar, the remaining coffee mixture and chopped walnuts.

4 Unroll the Swiss roll and spread with the cream. Tightly reroll and place on a long plate. Decorate with dots of cream and extra walnuts.

CHOCOLATE AND GINGER SWISS ROLL

4 large eggs, at room temperature
100g (4 oz) caster sugar
75g (3 oz) self-raising flour
25g (1 oz) cocoa powder
300ml (½ pint) double cream
6 bulbs stem ginger from a jar, chopped
100g (4 oz) Bournville chocolate, melted

1 Make the sponge as above (steps 1–3) and add the cocoa powder at the same time as the flour. Bake, cool and roll as above.

2 Whisk the cream until soft peaks then fold in the chopped ginger (reserve some for decoration).

3 Unroll the Swiss roll and spread with the cream. Tightly reroll and place on a long plate.

4 Drizzle the melted chocolate over the top in a zig-zag and sprinkle with the remaining pieces of ginger.

LEMON SWISS ROLL

4 large eggs, at room temperature
100g (4 oz) caster sugar
100g (4 oz) self-raising flour
finely grated zest of 1 lemon
300ml (½ pint) double cream
3 tablespoons quality lemon curd

1 Make the sponge as above (steps 1–3) but do not put the mixture in the tin.

2 Add the grated lemon zest to the sponge mixture and fold in. Bake, cool and roll as above.

3 Whisk the cream until soft peaks then fold in the lemon curd to give a marbled effect.

4 Unroll the Swiss roll and spread with the cream. Tightly reroll and place on a long plate.

Special Scones

The secret of good scones is not to have the mixture too dry – it should feel a bit sticky. Don't handle the dough too much, either – cut out quickly and bake. Use self-raising wholewheat flour, if you prefer; you will find that you need a little more milk.

225g (8 oz) self-raising flour
1 level teaspoon baking powder
40g (1½ oz) butter, softened
25g (1 oz) caster sugar
1 egg
about 150ml (¼ pint) milk

1 Lightly grease the cold plain shelf.

2 Measure the flour and baking powder into a bowl, add the butter and rub in until the mixture resembles fine breadcrumbs. Stir in the sugar. Break the egg into a measuring jug, whisk lightly and then make up to 150ml (¼ pint) with the milk. Stir into the flour and mix to a soft dough.

3 Turn on to a lightly floured surface and knead gently. Roll out to 2cm (¼ in) thick. Cut into rounds with a 5cm (2 in) fluted cutter. Arrange on the greased plain shelf and brush the tops with a little milk.

4 Slide the shelf on to the third set of runners in the Roasting Oven and cook the scones for about 10 minutes or until pale golden brown. Lift off the shelf and leave to cool on a wire rack.

5 Serve with clotted cream and strawberry jam.

PREPARE AHEAD
Best eaten on the day of making. If keeping for longer, refresh in the Simmering Oven on a baking tray for about 15 minutes until hot. These freeze extremely well for up to 6 months. Reheat as above.

CONVENTIONAL OVEN
Bake in an oven preheated to 220°C/Fan 200°C/Gas 7 for about 10–15 minutes or until the scones are well risen and a pale golden brown.

Apricot and Pumpkin Seed Oat Bites

Perfect for a packed lunch or to keep in the cupboard for a rainy day. It is important to cut them while they are still warm; if they are left to get completely cold they will be too brittle.

100g (4 oz) butter
100g (4 oz) golden syrup
100g (4 oz) demerara
sugar
175g (6 oz) porridge oats
25g (1 oz) pumpkin seeds
75g (3 oz) dried ready to
eat apricots, snipped
into small pieces

1 Grease and line a 20cm (8 in) sandwich tin with baking parchment.

2 Measure the butter, syrup and sugar into a small pan. Melt on the Boiling Plate, stirring until runny.

3 Remove from the heat, stir in the oats, seeds and apricots, and mix well. Spoon into the tin and level the top with the back of a spoon.

4 With the grid shelf on the floor of the Baking Oven cook for about 15–20 minutes, until golden and just firm.

2 oven Bake on the grid shelf on the floor of the Roasting Oven with the cold plain shelf on the second set of runners for 12–15 minutes until golden and just firm.

5 Leave to cool for a couple of minutes and then cut into wedges.

PREPARE AHEAD
Can be made up to 3 days ahead and kept in an airtight container. Freezes well for up to 2 months.

CONVENTIONAL OVEN
Bake in an oven preheated to 180°C/Fan 160°C/Gas 4 for about 30 minutes.

Wicked Chocolate Brownies

These are expensive to make, but worth it, and are even better when kept for a couple of days. As with all chocolate brownies, expect the mixture to sink slightly after baking. These are so rich, you only need a small square.

275g (10 oz) butter, softened, or baking spread
375g (13 oz) caster sugar
4 eggs
75g (3 oz) cocoa powder
100g (4 oz) self-raising flour
1 × 100g (4 oz) packet of plain chocolate 'polka dots'

PREPARE AHEAD
Make ahead, cool, cut into squares and keep in an airtight container for up to 1 week. Freeze whole when completely cold for up to 6 months.

CONVENTIONAL OVEN
Cook in an oven preheated to 190°C/Fan 170°C/Gas 5 for about 40–45 minutes.

1 Line the small roasting tin with foil and grease well.

2 Put all the ingredients together into a bowl and mix until well blended. This can be done in a processor, mixing in the 'polka dots' by hand at the last minute. Spoon the mixture into the roasting tin and level the top.

3 Put the grid shelf on the floor of the Baking Oven, and bake the brownie mixture for about 25 minutes, making sure the top does not get too dark. If it does, slip the cold plain shelf above on the second set of runners for the last 5 minutes. Then transfer the roasting tin to the centre of the Simmering Oven for a further 20 minutes or so, until a skewer comes out clean when inserted into the centre of the cake.

2 oven Put the tin on the grid shelf on the floor of the Roasting Oven with the cold plain shelf above on the second set of runners, and bake for about 25 minutes until set. Then very carefully transfer the now-hot plain shelf to the middle of the Simmering Oven and bake the brownies on it for about a further 20 minutes, or until a skewer comes out clean when inserted into the centre of the cake.

4 Cool in the tin. Remove the foil and cake from the tin. Store wrapped in more foil, or in a cake tin in the larder. Cut into squares to serve.

American Chocolate and Orange Muffins

If you are a real chocoholic you can double up on the chocolate drops! Use plain, milk or white chocolate.

225g (8 oz) self-raising
   flour
1 teaspoon baking
   powder
25g (1 oz) cocoa powder
100g (4 oz) light
   muscovado sugar
100g (4 oz) chocolate
   drops
1 egg
175ml (6 fl oz) milk
75ml (2½ fl oz)
   sunflower oil
finely grated zest
   of 1 orange

1 Line a 12-hole muffin tin with paper cases.

2 Measure all the ingredients into a bowl and beat well with a wooden spoon or with an electric beater until smooth. Distribute evenly among the paper cases.

3 Bake on the grid shelf on the floor of the Roasting Oven with the cold plain shelf on the second set of runners for about 15–20 minutes until well risen and cooked through.

4 Remove from the oven and leave to cool on a wire rack.

PREPARE AHEAD
Best eaten freshly made but you could pack and freeze the muffins for up to 4 months.

CONVENTIONAL OVEN
Bake in an oven preheated to 200°C/Fan 180°C/Gas 6 for 20–25 minutes.

Winter Welshcakes

Very easy to make from store-cupboard ingredients, and they
are wonderful for tea on a cold day. Make when you've had
a good cooking session in the Aga and the temperature is down.
Traditionally they are served plain with caster sugar but,
if liked, can be served with butter and jam.

350g (12 oz) self-raising
   flour
2 teaspoons baking
   powder
175g (6 oz) butter
115g (4¼ oz) caster
   sugar
100g (4 oz) currants
1 level teaspoon ground
   mixed spice
1 egg
about 2 tablespoons
   milk
a little caster sugar,
   for dusting

1 Lift the lid of the Simmering Plate to cool the plate
for about 10 minutes (depending on the heat of your
Simmering Plate).

2 Meanwhile, measure the flour and baking powder
into a large bowl and rub in the butter until the
mixture resembles fine breadcrumbs. Add the sugar,
currants and spice. Beat the egg with the milk then
add this to the mixture to form a firm dough.

3 Roll out the dough on a lightly floured work surface
to a thickness of 5mm (¼ in) and cut into rounds with
a 7.5cm (3 in) plain round cutter. Re-roll the trimmings
and continue pressing out with the cutter.

4 Grease the Simmering Plate lightly with oil or place
an ungreased sheet of non-stick paper over it. Cook
the Welshcakes for about 3 minutes on each side until
golden brown. (Be careful not to cook the cakes too
fast, otherwise they will not be cooked through.)

5 Cool on a wire rack, then dust with caster sugar.

PREPARE AHEAD
Best made and eaten on the day.

CONVENTIONAL OVEN
Heat and lightly grease a
griddle or heavy-based frying
pan (preferably non-stick).
Cook the Welshcakes on
a low heat for about 3 minutes
on each side until golden
brown and cooked through.

Chocolate Éclairs

Fill them with cream just before serving.

CHOUX PASTRY

50g (2 oz) butter
150ml (¼ pint) water
60g (2½ oz) flour
2 eggs, beaten

FILLING

300ml (½ pint)
  whipping cream,
  whipped
a few drops vanilla
  extract

ICING

150g (5 oz) dark
  Bournville chocolate
150ml (5 fl oz) double
  cream

PREPARE AHEAD

The choux pastry cases can
be made ahead and kept in an
airtight container for 2 days.
Fill and ice to serve.

CONVENTIONAL OVEN

Bake in an oven preheated to
220°C/Fan 200°C/Gas 7 for
10 minutes, then reduce the
temperature to 190°C/Fan
170°C/Gas 5 and bake for a
further 20 minutes, until well
risen and a deep golden brown.
Remove the éclairs from the
oven and split them down
one side to allow the steam to
escape. Leave to cool completely
on a wire rack. The chocolate
icing can be made in a bowl
over a pan of simmering water.

1 Grease two baking sheets.

2 Melt the butter in a pan with the water and slowly
bring to the boil, making sure all the butter has melted.
Remove from the heat and quickly add the flour all at
once and beat with a wooden spoon until it forms a ball
and looks all shiny. Gradually beat in the eggs a little
at a time to give a smooth paste. Put the mixture into
a piping bag fitted with a 1cm (½ in) nozzle and pipe
into 8cm (4 in) lengths on the baking trays, leaving
room in between for them to expand.

3 Slide on to the lowest set of runners in the
Roasting Oven and cook for about 20 minutes
until light golden brown.

4 When cool enough to handle split the éclairs down
one side with a sharp knife to let the steam escape,
placing them back on the baking sheets.

5 Transfer to the Simmering Oven for about
20 minutes until they are completely dry inside.

6 For the filling, mix the whipped cream with the
vanilla extract and pipe or spoon into the middle
of the éclairs.

7 To make the icing, break the chocolate into a bowl,
pour over the cream and sit on the back of the Aga
to melt, stirring occasionally, until combined and
glossy. Set aside to cool for a little and to thicken.
Dip the éclairs into the chocolate and leave to set
on a wire tray.

Chocolate and Ginger Oat Cookies

These cookies have a lovely crisp edge and squidgy middle. Watch carefully as they are dark from the chocolate so they can catch easily.

125g (4½ oz) butter, softened

150g (5 oz) light muscovado sugar

1 egg

½ teaspoon vanilla extract

2 teaspoons ground ginger

150g (5 oz) plain flour

75g (3 oz) porridge oats

100g (4 oz) dark chocolate chips

50g (2 oz) stem ginger from a jar, finely chopped

TO DECORATE

50g (2 oz) dark chocolate, melted

1 Line two baking sheets with baking parchment.

2 Measure the butter and sugar into a mixing bowl. Beat by hand or with an electric whisk until light and fluffy and pale in colour. Add the egg, vanilla, ground ginger, flour and oats. Whisk until well combined. Stir in the chocolate chips and chopped ginger.

3 Shape the dough into 24 balls. Place 12 balls on each baking sheet, well spaced apart, and press the centre of each down slightly.

4 Slide on to the grid shelf on the floor of the Roasting Oven with the cold plain shelf on the second set of runners for about 10 minutes or until golden.

5 Transfer to a wire rack to cool and then drizzle a zig-zag of melted chocolate over each cookie to serve.

PREPARE AHEAD
Can be made up to 2 days ahead and stored in an airtight container. The cookies also freeze well.

CONVENTIONAL OVEN
Bake in an oven preheated to 180°C/Fan 160°C/Gas 4 for about 10 minutes.

Classic Scottish Shortbread

Take care to cook through the underneath of the shortbread. It should be a very pale biscuit colour and not at all soggy. Using semolina gives a lovely crunch, but if you don't have semolina, use cornflour instead. To make less, halve the ingredients and use the small roasting tin.

350g (12 oz) plain flour
175g (6 oz) semolina
175g (6 oz) caster sugar
350g (12 oz) butter
25g (1 oz) demerara sugar

PREPARE AHEAD
Keep the shortbread in an airtight container for up to 1 week. It will also freeze for up to 2 months.

CONVENTIONAL OVEN
Bake in the oven preheated to 160°C/Fan 140°C/Gas 3, for about 35 minutes until pale golden and cooked through. All ovens vary so keep a strict eye on the shortbread.

VARIATIONS
WHOLEWEAT
Use 175g (6 oz) wholewheat flour instead of half the plain flour.

LEMON
Add the grated rind of 2 lemons.

GINGER
Take out 1 tablespoon of flour and add 1 tablespoon of ground ginger.

1 Measure the flour, semolina, caster sugar and butter into a processor and process until thoroughly combined. (This can be done by hand, rubbing the butter into the flour and semolina first, then adding the other ingredients and working together to form a ball.)

2 Press the shortbread mixture into the large roasting tin and level with the back of a spoon so that the mixture is the same depth all the way across. Sprinkle with the demerara sugar.

3 Bake in the Baking Oven on the lowest set of runners for 10 minutes. Slide in the cold plain shelf on the second set of runners for a further 15 minutes, then transfer to the Simmering Oven for a further 10–15 minutes until cooked.

 2 oven Slide the tin on to the lowest set of runners in the Roasting Oven with the cold plain shelf on the second set of runners for about 10 minutes until a pale golden colour (turning round halfway through if necessary). Do watch very carefully. Transfer the tin to the Simmering Oven for a further 30–40 minutes until the shortbread is cooked through.

4 Remove from the oven and allow to cool for a few minutes, then gently cut across into 24 squares, and then cut each square in half diagonally. Carefully lift the triangles out and leave to cool on a wire rack.

Smashing Bara Brith

Bara Brith is the Welsh name for tea loaf. It is very
moist and fruity and doesn't crumble when sliced.

**Makes 2 x 450g (1 lb)
loaves**
175g (6 oz) currants
175g (6 oz) sultanas
225g (8 oz) light
   muscovado sugar
300ml (½ pint) hot tea
275g (10 oz) self-raising
   flour
1 egg, beaten

1 Measure the fruit and sugar into a bowl and pour
over the hot tea. Stir well, cover and leave to stand
overnight. Grease and line 2 × 450g (1 lb) loaf
tins with greased greaseproof paper.

2 Stir the flour and egg into the fruit mixture, mix
thoroughly and divide between the tins.

3 Place the grid shelf on the fourth set of runners
in the Baking Oven and put the loaf tins on this
shelf, one in front of the other. Cook for about 1 hour.
A skewer should come out clean when pierced into
the centre of the loaves.

2 oven With the grid shelf on the floor of the
Roasting Oven and the cold plain shelf on the second
set of runners, cook the loaves for about 30 minutes
until set and just beginning to brown. Then transfer
the now hot plain shelf to the centre of the Simmering
Oven, and very carefully move the loaves on to this
shelf for a further 30 minutes or until cooked through.

4 Turn out the loaves and leave to cool on wire racks.
Serve sliced with a little butter.

PREPARE AHEAD
These loaves keep well for
up to 1 week as they are so
moist. They will also freeze
for up to 3 months.

CONVENTIONAL OVEN
Bake in an oven preheated to
160°C/Fan 140°C/Gas 3 for
about 1 hour or until a skewer
inserted into the centre comes
out clean.

Banana and Yoghurt Cakes

It is tricky cooking 900g (2 lb) loaf tins in the Aga as the outside can tend to burn before it gets cooked in the middle, so we find it easier to cook 2 × 450g (1 lb) loaves – eat one and freeze one. No need for icing – just serve as it is with butter, if liked. A loaf domes naturally in the tin and the crack is part of the charm.

Makes 2 x 450g (1 lb) loaves

2 ripe bananas (roughly 200g/7 oz)
250g (9 oz) self-raising flour
100g (4 oz) butter, softened, or baking spread
175g (6 oz) light muscovado sugar
2 eggs
150ml (¼ pint) natural yoghurt
50g (2 oz) sultanas (optional)

1 Line 2 × 450g (1 lb) tins with a wide strip of baking paper, greased all over.

2 Measure the bananas into a bowl and mash with a fork. Add all the remaining ingredients and beat well with a wooden spoon or with an electric beater for about 2 minutes until blended and smooth. Divide between the two tins and level the tops.

3 Bake on the grid shelf on the floor of the Roasting Oven with the cold plain shelf on the second set of runners for about 20–25 minutes until perfect golden brown and well risen. Slide the now hot cold plain shelf into the centre of the Simmering Oven and sit the tins on top. Bake for a further 20–30 minutes until firm on top and a skewer comes out clean when inserted in the middle.

4 Leave to cool in the tins for about 10 minutes and then turn on to a wire rack.

PREPARE AHEAD
Can be made up to 2 days ahead. Also freezes well cooked.

CONVENTIONAL OVEN
Bake in an oven preheated to 160°C/Fan 140°C/Gas 3 for 40 minutes.

BREADMAKING

PROVING AND RISING

Stand dough away from draughts,
preferably at a temperature of 20°–30°C
(a work surface beside the Aga is ideal).

COVER DOUGH

When leaving to prove always cover
loosely with oiled clingfilm or an oiled
polythene bag.

PRE-WARM TINS AND BOWLS

For best results always put greased
bread tins to warm on the top of
the Aga. The same applies to bowls
and flour to a slightly lesser degree.

AMOUNT OF LIQUID

Brown flour generally absorbs
a little more water than white flour.

MIXERS AND PROCESSORS

Rubbing in and kneading can be done
perfectly successfully in a food mixer
– see its instruction book for timing.
Brown bread requires less kneading.
You can also make your bread using
a processor – follow the instructions,
being very careful not to overprocess.

DRIED YEAST

There are two main types of dried yeast:
Fermipan, sold under various trade
names, contains no artificial bread
improvers; and **fast-action** dried yeast,
which contains vitamin C (ascorbic acid).
Follow instructions carefully on the packet.

STICKY DOUGH

If the dough is a bit wet and sticky
put your hand in a polythene bag
and knead using the bag as a glove.

GLAZING

For a shiny top, glaze with an egg
wash (beaten egg with a little water).

White Bread

The constant warmth of the Aga is ideal for rising and proving and the perfect oven for the actual baking. To make a wholemeal or granary loaf use 350g (12 oz) wholemeal or granary flour and 100g (4 oz) of strong white flour, plus the remaining ingredients listed below. Follow the same method, but the rising and proving time will be a little longer. This recipe can be used to make 1 × 900g (2 lb) loaf or 1 large round – bake on the grid sheet on the floor of the Roasting Oven for 25–35 minutes.

**Makes 2 x 450g
(1 lb) loaves**
450g (1 lb) strong
    white flour
7g sachet of fast-
    action yeast
1 level teaspoon salt
40g (1½ oz) butter,
    melted but not hot
300ml (½ pint)
    tepid water

1 Grease 2 × 450g (1 lb) loaf tins.

2 To make by hand, measure the flour into a bowl, add the yeast and salt separately on opposite sides on top of the flour. Add the butter and three-quarters of the water. Mix together using a wooden spoon or your hands until you have a fairly sticky dough, adding the remaining water until all of the flour is incorporated (you might need a little more water for wholemeal or granary loaves). Knead on a lightly floured work surface for about 10 minutes until the dough is smooth and soft. If using a free-standing mixer fitted with a dough hook, mix the ingredients in the bowl attached to the mixer until you have a fairly sticky, soft dough. Continue to knead until the dough is smooth and soft. This will take 5 minutes.

3 Transfer the dough to a large oiled bowl, cover tightly with clingfilm (make sure no air can escape) and leave to rise near the Aga for 1–1½ hours or until the dough has doubled in size.

Continued overleaf

Recipe continued

4 Put the greased tin near the Aga to warm, tip the dough out on to a floured work surface and knock back by hand until smooth (or put into the mixer and knead for 3 minutes using the dough hook). Divide the dough into two and slightly flatten the balls of dough with the heel of your hand and fold in two opposite sides, slightly overlapping, and roll up like a Swiss roll. With the fold underneath put in the loaf tins, place the tins on a baking sheet and put the baking sheet and tins into a large plastic bag. Seal the end to create a steamy atmosphere and leave to prove for about 30 minutes or until they have doubled in size and look springy. (With brown bread, as soon as a few 'pin' holes begin to appear, the loaf is ready to bake – the proving will take about 45 minutes–1 hour.) Remove the bag and dust the loaves with flour. Make three slashes on top of each loaf.

5 With the grid shelf on the floor of the Roasting Oven bake for about 25–35 minutes, until evenly browned and the bread sounds hollow when tapped on the base. Remove from the tins and leave to cool on a wire rack.

TIP
For a crown loaf, use the dough to make 12 equal-sized balls and place in a greased 20cm (8 in) shallow cake tin and bake for 25 minutes.

PREPARE AHEAD
Can be made a day ahead and freezes well for up to 2 months.

CONVENTIONAL OVEN
Bake in an oven preheated to 220°C/Fan 200°C/Gas 7, for about 25–30 minutes until golden and the bread sounds hollow when tapped on the base.

Irish Soda Bread

Quick to make and often baked fresh for breakfast or tea.

**Makes 1 x 450g
(1 lb) loaf**

450g (1 lb) plain flour
(or a mixture of
wholemeal and plain
flour)
1 level teaspoon
bicarbonate of soda
1 teaspoon salt
about 300–450ml
(½–¾ pint) buttermilk

1 Lightly grease a baking tray.

2 Mix the dry ingredients together. Add the buttermilk to form a very soft dough.

3 Turn the dough out on to a lightly floured work surface and shape into a neat round about 18cm (7 in) in diameter. Place on the baking tray and make a deep cross in the top with a sharp knife.

4 With the grid shelf on the floor of the Roasting Oven, bake for 30–35 minutes, turning once. When baked the loaf will sound hollow if tapped on the base. Wrap in a clean tea towel to cool – this stops the crust hardening too much.

PREPARE AHEAD
The bread is best made on the day but will freeze for up to 2 months.

CONVENTIONAL OVEN
Bake in an oven preheated to 200°C/Fan 180°C/Gas 6, for about 30 minutes, then turn the bread upside down and continue baking for about 10–15 minutes or until the bread sounds hollow when tapped on the bottom.

HOT PUDDINGS AND COLD DESSERTS

Tarte Tatin

Louis XIV's personal baker Monsieur Tatin had two daughters who made their father a caramelised upside-down apple pie using dessert apples. The King was so impressed with the tart that he always had it on his menu.

PASTRY
100g (4 oz) flour
50g (2 oz) butter,
    cut into cubes
1 level tablespoon
    icing sugar
1 egg yolk
scant tablespoon water

TOPPING
900g (2 lb) Cox's
    dessert apples
finely grated rind
    and juice of 1 lemon
75g (3 oz) butter
75g (3 oz) light
    muscovado sugar

1 Make the pastry either by hand using the usual rubbing-in method or by machine in a mixer or processor. Measure the flour, butter and icing sugar into a bowl and mix until it resembles fine breadcrumbs. Add the egg yolk and enough water to bring the mixture together to a firm but not sticky dough. Knead lightly, wrap in clingfilm and chill for about 30 minutes.

2 Meanwhile, peel, core and thickly slice the apples and sprinkle with the lemon juice and rind. Measure the butter and sugar into a heavy pan. Gently melt together without boiling on the Simmering Plate, until the sugar has dissolved, stirring occasionally. Add the apples, lemon juice and rind to the sugar mixture, and stir well until all the apples are coated. Tip or arrange the apples and juices into a lightly greased 20cm (8 in) sandwich tin and leave to cool.

3 Roll out the chilled dough on to a lightly floured surface and use to cover the apples. Trim off any surplus pastry.

4 With the grid shelf on the second set of runners, cook in the Baking Oven for about 30 minutes, until the pastry is crisp and golden brown.

2 oven With the grid shelf on the floor of the Roasting Oven and the cold plain shelf on the second set of runners, bake for about 20–25 minutes until the pastry is crisp and golden brown.

5 Remove from the oven (the pastry will have shrunk a little) and tip all of the juices from the tin into a small pan. Turn the tart out on to a plate, with the pastry on the bottom. Reduce the juices on the Boiling Plate for 3–4 minutes to a syrupy caramel and then pour over the apples. Serve warm or cold with lightly whipped cream.

TIP
You can make pastry with butter (or other fat) straight from the freezer. The secret is to grate it straight into the flour. This benefits the pastry doubly – the fat is extremely cold, as well as being in very small pieces.

PREPARE AHEAD
Can be made up to 6 hours ahead and served cold.

CONVENTIONAL OVEN
Cook in an oven preheated to 200°C/Fan 180°C/Gas 6 for about 20 minutes, until the pastry is crisp and golden brown.

Tarte au Citron

If using a metal flan tin with a loose bottom, take great care once the flan tin has been lined with pastry not to push the loose bottom upwards or sideways as it will puncture the pastry. Use a bought 500g (18 oz) pack of shortcrust pastry if time is short.

PASTRY

225g (8 oz) plain flour
100g (4 oz) butter, cut
  into cubes
50g (2 oz) caster sugar
1 egg

LEMON FILLING

9 eggs
300ml (10 fl oz) double
  cream
finely grated rind and
  juice of 5 large lemons
375g (13 oz) caster
  sugar

TO FINISH

a little icing sugar

PREPARE AHEAD

Line the tin or dish with pastry about 24 hours ahead, cover with clingfilm and put in the fridge.

CONVENTIONAL OVEN

Bake the pastry blind in an oven preheated to 200°C/ Fan 180°C/Gas 6. Lower the temperature to 180°C/Fan 160°C/Gas 4, pour the filling into the pastry case and bake for about 35–40 minutes until the lemon filling is set. Cover the tart loosely with foil if the pastry begins to brown too much.

1 Make the pastry either by hand using the usual rubbing-in method or by machine in a mixer or processor. Measure the flour and butter into a bowl and mix until it looks like breadcrumbs, add the sugar and mix for a moment, then add the egg and mix well until it holds together. Ideally rest in the fridge for 30 minutes. Use the pastry to line a 26cm (10½ in) flan tin. Prick the base with a fork and freeze for about 30 minutes until hard.

2 To make the filling, beat the eggs in a bowl, add the cream, lemon rind, juice and caster sugar, and mix until smooth. Pour the lemon mixture into the pastry case.

3 Bake on the floor of the Roasting Oven, with the cold plain shelf on the second set of runners, for about 30 minutes, watching carefully. After about 15 minutes, if the pastry is golden and the filling is just set, place a greased tent of foil over the tart. The tart may need turning halfway through cooking.

4 When cool, sieve over a dusting of icing sugar to decorate and serve with a little single cream.

Old-fashioned Treacle Tart

This is an open-topped tart. You can use the trimmings
to make a lattice pattern on the top, if liked.

PASTRY

175g (6 oz) plain flour
75g (3 oz) butter,
    cut into cubes
about 2 good
    tablespoons
    cold water

FILLING

400g (14 oz) golden
    syrup
100g (4 oz) fresh white
    breadcrumbs
grated rind and juice
    of 1 lemon

1 Make the pastry either by hand using the usual
rubbing-in method or by machine in a mixer or
processor. Measure the flour into a bowl, add the
butter and mix until it resembles fine breadcrumbs.
Add sufficient cold water to make a firm dough. Roll
out the pastry and use to line a 20cm (8 in) shallow flan
tin or deep ovenproof plate or dish. Chill in the fridge
for about 15 minutes then prick the bottom with a fork.

2 Meanwhile, mix together all the ingredients for the
filling in a large ovenproof bowl. Put the bowl in the
Simmering Oven for about 10 minutes for the crumbs
to swell. Pour into the pastry case and level out.
Decorate with pastry trimmings, if using.

3 Bake on the floor of the Roasting Oven for about
25 minutes or until the pastry is golden brown.
Don't worry if the filling is still runny, it will
solidify as it cools.

4 Serve warm, rather than hot, with cream, custard,
crème fraîche, ice cream or all of them!

PREPARE AHEAD

The tart can be made up to
2 days ahead and reheated
for 10 minutes in the Roasting
Oven to serve.

CONVENTIONAL OVEN

Cook in an oven preheated
to 200°C/Fan 180°C/Gas 6
for about 25 minutes, until
the pastry is golden brown.

Double Crust Fruit Pie

The Aga cooks plate pies well, getting the pastry crisp top and bottom.

225g (8 oz) plain flour
100g (4 oz) butter,
  cut into cubes
about 3 tablespoons
  cold water
450–675g (1–1½ lb)
  prepared fruit
75–100g (3–4 oz)
  granulated sugar
milk, to glaze
demerara sugar,
  to finish

PREPARE AHEAD

The pie can be assembled
1 hour ahead. It can also be
baked ahead and reheated in
the Simmering Oven to serve.

CONVENTIONAL OVEN

Bake in an oven preheated
to 200°C/Fan 180°C/Gas 6
for about 40 minutes, until
the pastry is golden brown
and the fruit cooked through.

1 You will need a 23cm (9 in) deep enamel pie plate.

2 Make the pastry either by hand using the usual rubbing-in method or by machine in a mixer or processor. Measure the flour into a bowl, add the butter and mix until it resembles fine breadcrumbs. Add sufficient cold water to make a firm dough. Divide in two and use one half to line the pie plate. Chill in the fridge for about 15 minutes then prick the bottom with a fork.

3 Toss the fruit in the granulated sugar and pile into the centre of the plate.

4 Roll the second half of pastry into a circle to cover the pie. Damp the edges of the pastry in the plate and then top with the circle. Use any trimmings to decorate. Brush with a little milk to glaze and sprinkle with a little sugar – demerara looks best. Stand the pie in the large roasting tin.

5 Stand the tin on the floor of the Roasting Oven and cook for about 20–25 minutes until the pastry is golden brown. Turn the pie round in the tin once during cooking, if necessary. Transfer the tin to the top of the Simmering Oven and cook for a further 20 minutes to cook the fruit through.

Pear Frangipane Tart

This is a great tart to serve for a party. Always serve it warm. You could use a bought 500g (18 oz) pack of shortcrust pastry if time is short.

PASTRY

100 (4 oz) butter,
  cut into cubes
225g (8 oz) plain flour
25g (1 oz) icing sugar,
  sieved
1 egg, beaten

FILLING

175g (6 oz) soft butter
175g (6 oz) caster sugar
3 eggs, beaten
175g (6 oz) ground
  almonds
40g (1½ oz) plain flour
1 teaspoon almond
  extract
6–8 fresh, ripe Williams
  pears, peeled, cored
  and halved

TO FINISH

apricot jam, melted
  and sieved, for glaze
25g (1 oz) flaked
  almonds, toasted

1 If making the pastry by hand, rub the butter into the flour and icing sugar until the mixture resembles breadcrumbs, then stir in the beaten egg and bring together to form a dough. If making in a processor, combine the butter, flour and icing sugar in the bowl then process until the mixture resembles ground almonds. Pour in the beaten egg and pulse the blade until the dough starts to form a ball around the central stem. Form the pastry into a smooth flat cake, wrap in clingfilm and chill for 30 minutes or until manageable.

2 Make the filling in the unwashed processor. Cream the butter and sugar together, then gradually add the beaten eggs (do not worry if it looks curdled at this stage). Scrape down the sides of the bowl with a spatula. Add the ground almonds, flour and almond extract. Process for a few seconds until well incorporated. Leave this mixture in the fridge until required.

3 Roll out the chilled pastry on a lightly floured work surface and line a flan tin 28cm (11 in) in diameter, about 2.5cm (1 in) deep. If possible, chill for a further 30 minutes.

4 Spoon the frangipane mixture into the pastry case and level the top using a small palette knife. Arrange the pear halves, cut side down, attractively on the filling. Be sure to leave enough room between them to allow the frangipane mixture to rise.

Continued overleaf

Recipe continued

5 Lift the tin on to a baking sheet and bake on the floor of the Roasting Oven until pale golden, about 15–20 minutes. Then transfer to the centre of the Baking Oven until set and golden brown, another 15–20 minutes.

2 oven Lift the tin on to a baking sheet and bake on the floor of the Roasting Oven for 15–20 minutes until pale golden. After this time put the cold plain shelf on the second set of runners and continue to bake for a further 15–20 minutes until the almond filling is set and golden brown. If the pastry is becoming too dark, place a ring of foil around the edge.

6 Cool slightly, brush with hot apricot glaze and sprinkle with toasted flaked almonds. Serve warm with cream or crème fraîche.

PREPARE AHEAD
The pastry-lined flan tin can be kept, covered with clingfilm, in the fridge for up to 24 hours. Filled with the frangipane mixture it can be kept for about 1 hour, covered and refrigerated. Alternatively, complete the tart to the end of step 5, cool, wrap and freeze for up to 1 month. To reheat, loosely cover the tart with foil and reheat in the Roasting Oven on the grid shelf on the floor for about 15 minutes.

CONVENTIONAL OVEN
Put a heavy flat baking tray into the oven to preheat. Place the tart on the tray and bake at 190°C/Fan 170°C/Gas 5 for about 45–50 minutes until the almond filling and pastry are golden brown. Complete step 6 as above.

Lemon Meringue Pie

This is such a favourite with both our families. Ped, Lucy's husband, was delighted by the taste testing he had to do! Generally, in the Aga we do not need to bake blind, and for a smaller LMP you may be able to bake directly on the floor of the oven, but for this large pie it is safer to bake the pastry blind first.

PASTRY

225g (8 oz) plain flour
25g (1 oz) icing sugar
150g (5 oz) butter,
  cut into cubes
1 egg
2 tablespoons water

FILLING

5 large lemons
75g (3 oz) cornflour
450ml (¾ pint) water
5 egg yolks
225g (8 oz) caster sugar

MERINGUE

5 egg whites
300g (10 oz) caster
  sugar

1 You will need a 28cm (11 in) deep, fluted, loose-bottomed flan tin.

2 Make the pastry either by hand using the usual rubbing-in method or by machine in a mixer or processor. Measure the flour and icing sugar into a bowl and mix in the butter until it resembles fine breadcrumbs. Add the egg and water and mix together until combined into a ball. Roll out the pastry on a floured work surface and line the flan tin along the base and sides. Prick the base with a fork and chill for 30 minutes.

3 Line the flan tin with greaseproof paper and baking beans and bake on the grid shelf on the floor of the Roasting Oven for 10 minutes. Remove the beans and the paper and return to the floor for another 5 minutes until lightly golden.

4 For the filling, finely grate the rinds from the lemons and squeeze out the juice. Put the rind, juice and cornflour in a small bowl and blend together. Bring the water to the boil, then stir into the cornflour mixture. Pour into a saucepan and heat on the Simmering Plate, stirring, until you have a thick 'custard'.

Continued overleaf

Recipe continued

5 Mix the egg yolks and sugar together and stir into the custard. Heat on the Boiling Plate, whisking until it bubbles a couple of times. Remove from the heat, allow to cool a little and then spread into the pastry case.

6 For the meringue, whisk the egg whites on full speed until stiff then add the sugar, a little at a time, whisking hard all the time. When all the sugar has been added, pile the meringue on top of the lemon custard, taking care that there are no gaps.

7 Bake on the grid shelf on the floor of the Roasting Oven for 3–4 minutes, or until the meringue is golden, and then transfer to the Simmering Oven for about 20 minutes until set.

PREPARE AHEAD
Can be made up to 6 hours ahead and reheated in the Simmering Oven to serve.

CONVENTIONAL OVEN
Bake the pastry blind in an oven preheated to 200°C/ Fan 180°C/Gas 6. Reduce the temperature to 150°C/Fan 130°C/Gas 2 and bake the pie for about 1 hour, until the meringue is crisp and pale beige on the outside and soft in the middle.

Apple and Lemon Tart

This is quite the best apple tart we know. A deep shell of crisp, buttery pastry, filled with a magical mixture that is like tarte au citron combined with grated apples. It freezes well too! If you haven't time to arrange the dessert apples on the top, don't worry, it will taste the same!

PASTRY

100g (4 oz) butter,
    cut into cubes
225g (8 oz) plain flour
25g (1 oz) icing sugar,
    sieved
1 egg, beaten
2 tablespoons water

FILLING

4 eggs
225g (8 oz) caster sugar
grated rind and juice
    of 2 lemons
100g (4 oz) butter,
    melted
2 large cooking apples,
    quartered, cored
    and peeled (about
    350g/12 oz prepared
    weight)
2 dessert apples,
    quartered, cored,
    peeled and thinly
    sliced
about 25g (1 oz)
    demerara sugar

1 If making the pastry by hand, rub the butter into the flour and icing sugar until the mixture resembles breadcrumbs, then stir in the beaten egg and bring together to form a dough. If making in a processor, combine the butter, flour and icing sugar in the bowl then process until the mixture resembles breadcrumbs. Pour in the beaten egg and pulse the blade until the dough starts to form a ball around the central stem. Form the pastry into a smooth ball, put inside a plastic bag and chill in the fridge for 30 minutes. Roll out and line a round deep flan tin about 28 × 4cm (11 × 1½ in) in the usual way, forming a small lip round the edge. Chill the tin for a further 30 minutes.

2 To prepare the filling, beat the eggs, caster sugar, lemon rind and juice together in a large mixing bowl. Stir in the warm melted butter then coarsely grate the cooking apples directly into the mixture and mix well. Have ready the thinly sliced dessert apples.

3 Remove the tart tin from the fridge and spread the runny lemon mixture in the base. Level the surface with the back of a spoon and arrange the dessert apple slices around the outside edge, neatly overlapping. Sprinkle the apple slices with demerara sugar.

4 Slide the tart on to the floor of the Roasting Oven and bake for about 10–15 minutes until the pastry is golden brown, then slide in the cold plain shelf on the second set of runners and bake for a further 15–20 minutes until the apple slices are tinged brown. Transfer to the Simmering Oven for a further 10 minutes until the filling is set.

PREPARE AHEAD

Line the tart tin with pastry, cover and keep in the fridge for up to 8 hours. Prepare the filling and keep covered in the fridge for up to 4 hours. Alternatively, to freeze, line the tart tin base with a circle of Lift-Off paper or non-stick baking paper before the pastry goes in. (This will guard against any acid from the filling reacting with the metal.) Remove the metal collar from the cooled baked tart. Wrap the tart carefully in clingfilm and seal inside a plastic bag. Freeze for up to 1 month. To reheat, put back into the metal flan tin and place in the Roasting Oven on the grid shelf on the floor for about 15 minutes.

CONVENTIONAL OVEN

Put a heavy baking tray into the oven to preheat, then bake the tart at 200°C/Fan 180°C/Gas 6, for about 40–50 minutes or until the centre feels firm to the touch and the apple slices are tinged brown.

Apple Crumble

For most Aga owners crumble is one of the great Sunday lunch puddings. So quick to make and quite wonderful to eat. Vary the fruit as the seasons come round: rhubarb, gooseberries, blackcurrants, plums etc. If using frozen fruit, measure out the amount you need then put it in a dish at the back of the Aga until just thawed. If you are in a hurry, thaw the fruit in the Simmering Oven for about 30 minutes – but do keep an eye on it! If you are using cooked fruit, only cook the crumble for 25–30 minutes in the Roasting Oven.

CRUMBLE
225g (8 oz) plain flour
100g (4 oz) butter
50g (2 oz) demerara
  sugar

FRUIT
1kg (2¼ lb) Bramley
  cooking apples, peeled
  and thickly sliced
175g (6 oz) caster sugar
1 teaspoon cinnamon

1 You will need a 1.4 litre (2½ pint) shallow dish.

2 Measure the flour into a bowl, add the butter and rub until the mixture resembles breadcrumbs. Stir in the demerara sugar.

3 Toss the prepared fruit in the caster sugar and cinnamon to cover. Tip the fruit into the dish and level out. Sprinkle the crumble over the top.

4 Slide the dish on to the second set of runners in the Roasting Oven and cook for about 25–30 minutes, then transfer to the top of the Simmering Oven for about 40 minutes, until the crumble is cooked through and the fruit is soft.

5 Serve with cream or custard.

PREPARE AHEAD
Prepare the crumble up to 12 hours ahead. It also freezes well uncooked.

CONVENTIONAL OVEN
Cook in an oven preheated to 200°C/Fan 180°C/Gas 6 for 35–40 minutes, until the crumble is cooked through and the fruit is soft.

Bread and Butter Pudding

Loved by all – for a change replace the currants and sultanas with other dried fruit. Ideally use an oblong dish as the bread fits in better. If you use thin sliced bread use twelve slices and you'll find you get three layers of bread instead of two.

about 8 medium slices of white bread, crusts removed
about 40g (1½ oz) butter, melted
100g (4 oz) currants and sultanas, mixed
grated rind of 1 lemon
50g (2 oz) caster or demerara sugar
2 eggs
1 teaspoon vanilla extract
450ml (¾ pint) milk

1 Well butter a 18 × 23cm (7 × 9 in) shallow ovenproof dish.

2 Cut each slice of bread into three. Take enough breadstrips to cover the base of the dish and dip each in melted butter on one side. Lay them in the prepared dish buttered side down. Sprinkle over the fruit, lemon rind and half the sugar. Cover with another layer of bread buttered side up.

3 Beat together the eggs, vanilla and milk and pour over the bread. Sprinkle with the remaining sugar and leave to stand for about an hour if time allows.

4 Place the dish on the grid shelf on the floor of the Baking Oven and cook for 25–30 minutes until crisp and golden brown and the pudding slightly puffed up.

 2 oven Place the dish on the grid shelf on the floor of the Roasting Oven with the cold plain shelf on the second runners down and cook for 25–30 minutes.

PREPARE AHEAD
You can prepare the pudding ahead of time and keep it covered in the fridge for up to 6 hours before baking. Don't sprinkle over the demerara sugar topping until 1 hour before you are ready to bake.

CONVENTIONAL OVEN
Cook in an oven preheated to 180°C/Fan 160°C/Gas 4 for about 30 minutes until crisp and golden.

Treacle Pudding

Quite an old-fashioned recipe but perfect for cooking in the Aga.

6 good tablespoons
    golden syrup
175g (6 oz) self-raising
    flour
50g (2 oz) caster sugar
75g (3 oz) shredded
    vegetable suet
1 teaspoon vanilla
    extract
about 150ml (¼ pint)
    milk

1 You will need a 1.1 litre (2 pint) pudding basin, greased.

2 Measure the golden syrup into the bottom of the basin.

3 Mix the flour, sugar and suet together in a mixing bowl. Add the vanilla extract and enough milk to bind to a soft dough. Pour into the basin on top of the syrup. Cover with greaseproof paper and seal the top with a foil lid.

4 Put the basin in a stainless steel saucepan with a tight-fitting lid. Fill with enough water to come halfway up the basin and bring to the boil on the Boiling Plate for about 8 minutes.

5 Transfer the pan, water and basin to the floor of the Simmering Oven and cook for about 3½ hours until the pudding is nicely risen and firm to the touch.

6 Turn the pudding upside down on to a plate so that all the syrup runs down the sides. Serve warm with custard and more warm golden syrup, if liked.

PREPARE AHEAD
The pudding can be prepared a day ahead.

CONVENTIONAL OVEN
Cook on the hob for about 3½ hours, occasionally checking on the level of the water in the pan, topping up when needed with more boiling water.

Proper Custard

Homemade proper custard is simply delicious, although it can be prone to curdling, so we add a teaspoon of cornflour which prevents this. If you are brave leave it out. Mary has a Kilner jar full of caster sugar and a few split vanilla pods sitting in her cupboard, which gives vanilla sugar, and you can use this instead of the sugar and extract listed below. For a richer custard use single cream instead of milk.

Makes 300ml (½ pint)
300ml (½ pint) full-fat
   milk
3 egg yolks or
   2 whole eggs
a few drops vanilla
   extract
1 tablespoon caster
   sugar
1 level teaspoon
   cornflour

1 Heat the milk in a small pan on the Boiling Plate until it almost boils.

2 Beat the egg yolks (or whole eggs), vanilla, sugar and cornflour together in a small bowl, pour on the hot milk, stirring thoroughly the whole time.

3 Return the custard to the pan and heat gently on the Simmering Plate for about a minute or two until it puckers or is hand hot, and thinly coats the back of a spoon. Strain if liked. Can be served hot, warm or cold.

PREPARE AHEAD
Can be made up to a day ahead and served cold, or made 1 hour ahead and kept warm on the back of the Aga.

CONVENTIONAL OVEN
Cook on the hob in the usual way.

Rice Pudding

We have to confess that no two rice puddings ever turn out
the same but they are always good! If you are in a hurry,
heat the milk and it will cook quicker.

100g (4 oz) pudding rice
50g (2 oz) caster sugar
1.2 litres (2 pints) full-
   fat milk
1 teaspoon vanilla
   extract
grated nutmeg
a knob of butter

1 Butter a 1.8 litre (3 pint) shallow ovenproof dish.

2 Scatter the rice into the base of the dish. Sprinkle
with the sugar and pour in the milk and vanilla. Stir
gently and then dust with nutmeg and dot with butter.

3 Slide on to the lowest shelf in the Roasting Oven for
about 45 minutes, or until browned. Carefully transfer
to the Simmering Oven for about 2–2½ hours or until
the rice has absorbed all the milk and is tender.

PREPARE AHEAD
Best cooked to serve.

CONVENTIONAL OVEN
Cook in an oven preheated
to 140°C/Fan 120°C/Gas 2
for about 2–2½ hours, or until
the rice is tender.

Hot Lemon Soufflé

A simple sauce to go with this pudding can be made by combining natural yoghurt with 2 tablespoons lemon curd and a little lemon juice.

40g (1½ oz) butter
40g (1½ oz) flour
300ml (½ pint) milk,
    less 3 tablespoons
grated rind and juice
    of 2 lemons
4 large eggs
75g (3 oz) caster sugar

1 Grease a 600ml (1 pint) straight-sided pudding basin or soufflé dish.

2 Melt the butter in a pan on the Boiling Plate. Add the flour and cook for a minute, then gradually whisk in the milk and bring to the boil, stirring until thickened. Stir in the grated lemon rind and juice and leave to cool.

3 Separate the eggs and beat the yolks one at a time into the lemon mixture. Add the sugar.

4 Whisk the egg whites until they are stiff but not dry. Stir 1 tablespoon into the lemon mixture then carefully fold in the remainder. Pour into the prepared dish.

5 Bake on the lowest set of runners in the Baking Oven for 30 minutes until well risen and golden brown. The very middle of the soufflé will still have a wobble. If you like it firm cook for a little longer.

2 oven With the grid shelf on the floor of the Roasting Oven and the cold plain shelf on the second set of runners, cook the soufflé for about 25 minutes until well risen and golden brown.

PREPARE AHEAD
You can bake the pudding ahead and then reheat for 15 minutes in a roasting tin of water in the Baking Oven, or for 10 minutes in the Roasting Oven, to serve.

CONVENTIONAL OVEN
Cook in an oven preheated to 190°C/Fan 170°C/Gas 5 for 30 minutes until well risen and golden brown.

Double Chocolate Puddings

This is a wonderful alternative pudding, which can be prepared ahead but is best cooked to serve straightaway.

50g (2 oz) cocoa powder, sifted
6 tablespoons boiling water
100ml (4 fl oz) milk
3 eggs
175g (6 oz) self-raising flour
1 rounded teaspoon baking powder
100g (4 oz) butter, softened, or baking spread
275g (10 oz) caster sugar
1 × 200g (7 oz) bar of plain chocolate, broken into squares
icing sugar, for dusting

1 Butter eight size 1 (9cm/3½ in) ramekins and line the bases with buttered greaseproof paper. No need to line the base if you are not turning them out.

2 Put the cocoa in the processor or mixer, set the machine in motion and carefully spoon in the boiling water. Blend for 1–2 minutes then scrape down the sides of the bowl and add the remaining cake ingredients, apart from the chocolate and icing sugar. Process again until the mixture has become a smooth, thickish batter. Divide the mixture between the prepared ramekins, and stack 4 squares of chocolate in the centre of each.

3 Bake on the grid shelf on the floor of the Baking Oven until the top of each pudding is firm and shrinking away from the sides of the dish, about 15 minutes.

2 oven Bake on the grid shelf on the floor of the Roasting Oven with the cold plain shelf on the second set of runners for 15 minutes, until the top of the pudding is firm and shrinking away from the sides of the dish.

4 Serve straight from the oven dusted with icing sugar or allow to settle for 4–5 minutes, turn out and dust with icing sugar. Serve with a little single cream.

PREPARE AHEAD
Prepare to the end of step 2 up to 24 hours ahead. Alternatively, freeze the raw mixture in the ramekins for up to 6 weeks. Bake as directed, allowing 2–3 minutes longer.

CONVENTIONAL OVEN
Cook in an oven preheated to 200°C/Fan 180°C/Gas 6 for about 15–20 minutes until firm and the pudding is shrinking away from the sides of the tin.

Passion Fruit and Lemon Cheesecake

A wonderful cooked cheesecake. Expect its centre to dip in the middle once cooked. If liked, you can add 175g (6 oz) sultanas to the cheesecake mixture with the egg whites before baking and, in this case, forget the decoration of fresh fruit.

BISCUIT BASE

75g (3 oz) digestive biscuits, crushed
40g (1½ oz) butter, melted but not hot
25g (1 oz) demerara sugar

CHEESECAKE

50g (2 oz) butter, softened
175g (6 oz) caster sugar
450g (1 lb) curd cheese or full-fat cream cheese
25g (1 oz) plain flour
finely grated rind and juice of 1 lemon
3 eggs, separated
150ml (5 fl oz) double cream, lightly whipped

TOPPING

4 passion fruit, halved
4 tablespoons lemon curd

1 Lightly grease a 23cm (9 in) loose-bottomed cake tin or spring-form tin, and line with greased greaseproof paper. You do need to line the tin as the mixture is slack when it goes into the tin and may seep through the bottom.

2 Mix together the ingredients for the base and spread over the base of the tin. Press down firmly with the back of a spoon.

3 Measure the butter, sugar, cheese, flour, lemon rind and juice and the egg yolks into a large bowl. Beat until smooth, then fold in the lightly whipped cream. Whisk the egg whites until stiff then fold into the mixture. Pour on to the crust in the tin.

4 Bake on the grid shelf on the floor of the Baking Oven for about 20 minutes until pale golden, then transfer to the centre of the Simmering Oven for a further 20 minutes until set.

2 oven Slide into the Roasting Oven on the grid shelf on the floor with the cold plain shelf on the second set of runners. Bake for 20 minutes. (If the top is not pale golden, remove the plain shelf from above and cook for a few more minutes.) Now transfer the very hot plain shelf to the centre of the Simmering Oven and place the cheesecake on top. Bake for a further 20 minutes until set.

Continued overleaf

Recipe Continued

5 Leave to cool in the tin – it will sink a little. Run a knife around the edge of the tin and lift out. Remove the paper and transfer to a serving plate. Using a teaspoon, scoop out the seeds from the passion fruit and mix with the lemon curd. Spoon over the top of the cold cheesecake.

6 Serve in wedges on its own or with slices of fresh mango.

TIP
To crush digestive biscuits or other biscuits for a cheesecake base, put into a clean polythene bag and roll firmly with a rolling pin. Or use a double thickness of polythene bags and *stand* on them until crushed! Very quick and easy.

PREPARE AHEAD
The cooked cheesecake can be made up to 2 days ahead – decorate with fruit on the day of serving. It also freezes well without decoration for up to 1 month.

CONVENTIONAL OVEN
Bake the cheesecake in an oven preheated to 160°C/Fan 140°C/Gas 3, for about 1 hour or until set. Turn off the oven and leave the cheesecake in the oven for a further hour to cool. Complete as in step 5.

Meringues

Aga meringues are quite wonderful – a beautiful creamy colour. If you like more toffee-flavoured ones, use half caster and half light muscovado sugar.

3 egg whites
175g (6 oz) caster sugar
a little demerara sugar
150ml (¼ pint)
   whipping cream

1 Line the cold plain shelf with a sheet of baking parchment.

2 Whisk the egg whites on full speed until they form soft peaks. Add the caster sugar, a teaspoonful at a time, whisking well.

3 Using two dessertspoons, spoon the meringue out on to the baking parchment – you should have 16 meringues. Dust with demerara sugar.

4 Slide on to the lowest runners in the Simmering Oven for about 2 hours, until the meringues are firm and dry and will lift easily from the baking parchment. If you like them very dry in the middle, after 1½ hours turn the meringues on their sides. (They will be pale off-white, or slightly darker if you have used muscovado sugar). Cool.

5 Whip the cream until it is thick and use this to sandwich the meringues together, or store them until required in an airtight tin.

PREPARE AHEAD
The meringues can be made up to 1 month ahead and kept in an airtight tin. Sandwich with cream to serve.

CONVENTIONAL OVEN
Cook in an oven preheated to 150°C/Fan 130°C/Gas 2 for an hour, switch off the oven and leave in the oven until cold.

Îles Flottantes

Such an ideal recipe for the Aga as the meringues are poached
in the Simmering Oven. Serve this with a red fruit salad –
the colours look magnificent – or simply on its own.

butter
3 eggs, separated
200g (7 oz) caster sugar
600ml (1 pint) milk
½ teaspoon vanilla
    extract
1 heaped teaspoon
    cornflour

1 Grease a shallow 23–25cm (9–10 in) shallow
ovenproof dish with butter. The dish must have
a large top surface to accommodate the meringues.

2 Whisk the egg whites at full speed in an electric
mixer for 1 minute, then add 175g (6 oz) of the sugar
gradually over several minutes, keeping the whisk
at full speed, until the meringue is stiff and glossy.

3 Bring the milk to the boil in a saucepan on the
Boiling Plate.

4 In a separate bowl mix the egg yolks, the remaining
caster sugar, the vanilla and cornflour. Using a balloon
whisk, pour over the boiling milk very slowly and whisk
all the time. Return the custard to the heat and cook
gently until the froth disappears and the custard is lightly
thickened. Pour the custard into the prepared dish.

5 Using 2 tablespoons, make oval shapes from the
meringue and arrange these on top of the custard.
The mixture should make about ten meringues.

6 Transfer the meringues and custard to the
Simmering Oven and bake for 15–20 minutes,
or until the meringues are set and no longer sticky
when lightly pressed with a finger. Serve warm.

PREPARE AHEAD
Can be cooked, cooled, covered
and kept in the fridge for up
to 2 days. The meringues
will shrink slightly during
this time.

CONVENTIONAL OVEN
Bake in an oven preheated
to 160°C/Fan 140°C/Gas 3
for about 20 minutes, until
the meringues are set and
no longer sticky.

Pistachio and Raspberry Pavlova with Butterscotch Sauce

The Aga makes very good Pavlovas and meringues, and they are such a great dessert for making ahead and for serving lots of people, as you can make them any shape or size you wish. It is so important to whisk the sugar well into the egg whites. You can use hazelnuts or almonds instead of pistachios, if you prefer.

PAVLOVA

4 egg whites
225g (8 oz) caster sugar
1 level teaspoon cornflour
1 teaspoon vinegar
50g (2 oz) pistachio nuts, roughly chopped
300ml (½ pint) double cream, whipped
350g (12 oz) fresh raspberries

BUTTERSCOTCH SAUCE

50g (2 oz) butter
50g (2 oz) muscovado sugar
150ml (¼ pint) double cream
1 teaspoon vanilla extract

1 Line a large baking sheet with non-stick baking paper and, using a pencil, mark out a 12 × 30cm (4½ × 12 in) rectangle.

2 Whisk the egg whites on high speed until they are like a cloud and then gradually add the caster sugar a teaspoonful at a time, whisking all the time. When the whites look shiny, thick and stiff, mix the cornflour and vinegar together in a tiny bowl and then pour into the meringue. Add the chopped nuts and stir everything together to combine.

3 Fit a piping bag with a plain nozzle and fill with the meringue. Twist to seal the top. Pipe along the lines of the rectangle and then along the base to give an even thickness of meringue. Pipe on top of the outer edges to build up the sides, in order to give a basket of meringue.

4 Slide the meringue on to the grid shelf on the floor of the Roasting Oven with the cold sheet on the second set of runners for about 3–5 minutes until lightly golden. Transfer to the Simmering Oven for 1–1½ hours or until easy to lift off the paper.

Continued overleaf

Recipe continued

5 Allow to cool on top of the Aga for about 30–45 minutes to dry out a little (a Pavlova middle should be soft). Peel away the paper and place on a serving plate.

6 Whisk the cream to soft peaks and spoon into the inside of the Pavlova, scattering the raspberries on top.

7 To make the butterscotch sauce, measure the butter, sugar and cream into a small pan and heat on the Boiling Plate. Stir until the butter has melted, and then bring to the boil, stirring all the time. Set aside to cool slightly and then drizzle over the raspberries and Pavlova walls to serve.

PREPARE AHEAD
The meringue can be made up to 1 month ahead and kept covered in a cool dry place. Fill with cream up to 4 hours before serving. Pour over the sauce just before serving.

CONVENTIONAL OVEN
Cook in an oven preheated to 150°C/Fan 130°C/Gas 2 for an hour, switch off the oven and leave the Pavlova in the oven until cold.

Lime Meringue Roulade

A meringue roulade is quicker and easier to make than a lemon meringue pie, and is just as popular. It freezes extremely well.

5 egg whites
275g (10 oz) caster
    sugar
50g (2 oz) flaked
    almonds, toasted

FILLING
300ml (½ pint) double
    cream
grated rind and juice of
    1 small lime
2 generous tablespoons
    lime or lemon curd

1 Line a 33 × 23cm (13 × 9 in) Swiss roll tin with greased non-stick baking paper. Secure the corners with four paper clips.

2 First make the meringue. Whisk the egg whites in an electric mixer on full speed until very stiff. Gradually add the sugar, a teaspoon at a time, still on high speed, whisking well between each addition. Whisk until very, very stiff and shiny, and all the sugar has been added.

3 Spread the meringue mixture into the prepared tin and sprinkle with the almonds.

4 Put the tin on the grid shelf on the floor of the Baking Oven and bake for about 8 minutes until pale golden. Transfer to the Simmering Oven and bake the roulade for a further 15 minutes until slightly crisp and firm to the touch. The roulade does expand, so take care of the edges when transferring.

2 oven Put the tin on the grid shelf on the floor of the Roasting Oven with the cold plain shelf on the second set of runners and bake for about 8 minutes until pale golden. Then transfer to the Simmering Oven, and bake the roulade for a further 15 minutes until slightly crisp and firm to the touch.

Continued overleaf

Recipe continued

5 Remove the meringue from the oven and turn almond side down on to a sheet of non-stick baking paper. Remove the paper from the base of the cooked meringue and allow to cool for about 10 minutes.

6 Lightly whip the cream, add the lime juice and all but a pinch of rind, and fold in the lime or lemon curd. Spread evenly over the meringue. Make an indentation 1cm (½ in) in on the long side with a knife, then roll up the meringue fairly tightly from the long end to form a roulade, allowing the paper to help you roll. It is essential to roll tightly and firmly at the beginning. Expect the roulade to crack – it is part of its charm.

7 Wrap in non-stick baking paper and chill well before serving. Sprinkle with the reserved lime rind to serve.

PREPARE AHEAD
The roulade can be made the day before it is needed. Complete to the end of step 6, wrap and keep in the fridge. Alternatively, this roulade also freezes well, stuffed and rolled, and so is perfect for entertaining. Wrap in foil and freeze for up to 2 months. Thaw the roulade for about 8 hours in the fridge.

CONVENTIONAL OVEN
Cook the meringue in an oven preheated to 220°C/ Fan 200°C/Gas 7 for about 12 minutes until golden. Then lower the temperature to 160°C/Fan 140°C/Gas 3 and bake for a further 15 minutes until firm to the touch.

The Ultimate Chocolate Roulade

Big, classic and brilliant! Using 10 eggs gives you a
massive chocolate roulade, perfect for special occasions.

275g (10 oz) plain
  Bournville chocolate
275g (10 oz) caster
  sugar
10 eggs, separated
50g (2 oz) cocoa
  powder, sieved

TO FINISH

450ml (16 fl oz)
  double cream
2 tablespoons Baileys
  cream liqueur or
  Kahlua liqueur
icing sugar

PREPARE AHEAD

Complete the roulade up to 24
hours ahead, cover and keep in
the fridge. Alternatively, wrap
and freeze the roulade for up
to 1 month.

CONVENTIONAL OVEN

Halve the recipe, unless you
have a huge cake tin. Bake the
roulade in a large Swiss roll
tin/roasting tin in the centre
of an oven preheated to 180°C/
Fan 160°C/Gas 4 for 25
minutes, or until firm to the
touch. Continue as above.

1 Grease and line the large Aga roasting tin with
non-stick baking paper. Break the chocolate into small
pieces into a bowl and stand the bowl on the back of
the Aga until the chocolate melts. Cool slightly.

2 Measure the sugar and egg yolks into a large bowl
and whisk with an electric whisk on high speed until
light and creamy. Add the cooled chocolate and stir
until evenly blended.

3 In a separate bowl, whisk the egg whites until stiff
but not dry. Carefully fold into the chocolate mixture.
Stir in the sieved cocoa powder and turn into the
prepared roasting tin and gently level the surface.

4 Hang the roasting tin on the lowest set of runners
in the Baking Oven, and bake for about 25 minutes,
turning after 18 minutes. If the roulade looks as though
it is browning too quickly, slide the cold plain shelf
on the second set of runners above the roulade.
When baked the roulade should be firm to the touch.
Remove from the oven and leave in the tin to cool.

2 oven Hang the tin on the lowest set of runners
in the Roasting Oven and slide the cold plain shelf
on the second set of runners above. Bake for about
25 minutes, turning after 18 minutes.

5 Meanwhile, whip the cream until it just holds its
shape and swirl in the cream liqueur.

6 Dust a large piece of greaseproof paper with sieved
icing sugar. Turn out the roulade and peel off the paper.
Spread with the cream. Score a mark 2.5cm (1 in) in
along the long edge. Roll up very tightly using the paper
to help. Do not worry when the roulade cracks – a good
one should! Dust with more sieved icing sugar to serve.

Crème Caramel

Make this custard the day before so it comes
out complete with the caramel.

CARAMEL
100g (4 oz) caster sugar

CUSTARD
4 eggs
1 teaspoon vanilla
    extract
600ml (1 pint) milk

1 Measure the caster sugar into a small pan, add water to cover. Dissolve the sugar stirring all the time, then boil rapidly without stirring until the caramel is a deep golden colour. Remove from the heat at once and carefully add 1 tablespoon of water to stop the caramel from cooking further. Take great care as it bubbles and spits fiercely at this point. Pour at once into a 1 litre (2 pint) soufflé dish.

2 Lightly whisk the eggs in a bowl with the vanilla extract. Heat the milk until hand hot then pour on to the eggs, stirring constantly.

3 Butter the sides of the dish above the caramel and strain the custard into the dish. Place the dish in the small roasting tin half filled with boiling water. Cover the top with a piece of foil.

4 Hang the tin on the lowest set of runners in the Roasting Oven for 15 minutes. Transfer the tin to the floor of the Simmering Oven for about 1 hour or until the custard is set.

5 Leave to get completely cold, preferably overnight in the fridge, before turning out.

PREPARE AHEAD
Best made a day ahead.

CONVENTIONAL OVEN
Cook in an oven preheated to
160°C/Fan 140°C/Gas 3 for
1 hour or until the custard is set.

Crème Brûlée

A classic and a favourite. As there is no grill in the Aga, you make
the caramel in a saucepan on the Boiling Plate and then pour it
on to the set custard. This gives shards of caramel, rather than
a thin layer. If you prefer the traditional way, sprinkle caster
sugar on the set custard and use a blow torch to brûlée.

4 egg yolks
1 teaspoon vanilla
   extract
25g (1 oz) caster sugar
600ml (1 pint) single
   cream

BRÛLÉE

100g (4 oz) caster sugar
8 tablespoons water

PREPARE AHEAD

The puddings can be made
to the end of step 3 up to
2 days ahead.

CONVENTIONAL OVEN

Cook the custards in a bain-
marie in an oven preheated
to 160°C/Fan 140°C/Gas 3
for 25–30 minutes or until
set. For the brûlée, preheat
the grill to hot. Sprinkle
the top of the custards with
the demerara sugar to about
5mm (¼ in) thickness and
place under the grill on a high
shelf until the sugar melts
then caramelises to a golden
brown. This takes 3–4 minutes.
Keep watch to make sure the
sugar does not burn.

1 Very lightly butter six size 1 (9cm/3½ in) ramekins.

2 Beat the egg yolks with the vanilla extract and caster
sugar until smooth.

3 Heat the cream in a pan on the Simmering Plate
to a hand hot temperature and gradually beat into
the egg yolk mixture.

4 Stand the ramekins in the small Aga roasting tin
then pour the egg yolk mixture through a sieve into
the dishes. Pour boiling water into the tin to come
halfway up the sides of the dishes.

5 Carefully push the tin on to the third set of runners
in the Roasting Oven and cook for about 10 minutes.
Carefully transfer the tin to the bottom set of runners
in the Simmering Oven and cook for a further 45
minutes until set. Lift out, leave to cool, then chill.

6 For the brûlée, measure the sugar and water into
a heavy pan and heat on the Simmering Plate, stirring
with a wooden spoon, until the sugar has dissolved.
Transfer to the Boiling Plate and bring to the boil
without stirring. Allow to boil steadily until the syrup
is pale golden brown. Remove from the heat and allow
to cool slightly, then pour over the top of the set
custards and allow to set. Chill again for a couple
of hours before serving.

INDEX

THANK YOUS FROM US BOTH

Huge, huge thank yous go to Lucinda McCord, once again, for all her help on this book – testing, retesting and triple checking the recipes. As ever she is a treasure to have by our sides.

Thanks to the Headline team, Jonathan Taylor, Muna Reyal, for commissioning the book, and lovely Jo Roberts-Miller who edits to perfection. It has been 16 years since Jo edited our first book so she knows our recipe style inside out and it's working with a friend. Thanks also to Felicity Bryan, our agent, who makes everything seamless.

Georgia Glynn Smith has taken stunning photos, with such a skilled eye and full of laughter and smiles, and had the help of Bobby Goulding who ate his way through every dish in this book, nearly before the camera had clicked! Thanks to Ellie Jarvis, Danielle Sanchez and Elayna Rudolphy for the delicious-looking food and making our recipes come to life.

Emma, Alex and Zoë at Smith and Gilmour have designed with style and grace – thanks for your attention to detail and the delicious homemade sausages on the shoot at Lucy's house!

William McGrath, CEO AGA Rangemaster Group plc, has embraced the book from day one. Dawn Roads is our technical guru and has been with Aga forever and her years of expertise have been invaluable to us. Laura James – the hub of Aga – is always at the end of the phone, keeping us up to date with what's going on, so thank you.

It's a joy to do our third joint book together and we hope you find every recipe you need and more.

Mary Berry   Lucy
x

Mary Berry is well known as the author of more than 70 cookery books with total sales of over 5 million. She has presented a number of television series and is currently a judge on *The Great British Bake Off*. She contributes to radio programmes and cookery magazines, and is loved for her practical and unfussy approach. Mary has had an Aga for over 40 years and, together with Lucy, ran Aga Workshops at home attended by some 14 thousand Aga owners. She loves to be with her family and tending their garden – her other great passion.

Lucy Young is Cordon Bleu trained and for the last 25 years has worked with Mary, testing recipes and teaching at her Aga Workshops. Mary describes Lucy as 'a truly exceptional cook' who will appeal to a whole new generation. Lucy's expertise is in creating and demonstrating no-hassle recipes to cook for family and friends. She is the author of seven books and this is the third that she has co-authored with Mary. Lucy lives at home with her husband, Ariel the cat and Frank and Matilda, their two pet ducks.

Mary has a 5 oven Aga and Lucy has an Aga Total Control - they are both duck egg blue! Mary and Lucy still work together every day and are great friends.